In This Place:
A Memoir

by Henry Neufeld

Published by:

FriesenPress
Suite 300 – 852 Fort Street
Victoria, BC, Canada V8W 1H8

www.friesenpress.com

Distributed to the trade by The Ingram Book Company

Table of Contents

Acknowledgements

In writing one's life story there is a realizations that our lives are entwined with numerous people, places, and events. All of these had an impact in shaping who we have become. When writing memoirs one cannot acknowledge everyone who has contributed to our life.

My greatest thanks go to my dear Tena for her encouragement and for her toleration of the time I spent in the "attic" researching and writing. Our children have encouraged me to write. Our daughter Bev helped design the cover page. The caricature on the back cover is by a Cuban artist.

Thanks to Henry Klippenstein, Jake Buhler and Dave Kroeker for the commentaries and editorial suggestions. Fortunately, over the years, we've collected and kept a lot of letters and documents and they were a helpful source of information and insight.

My apologies to those many friends whose names did not make it into this volume; your influence in our lives has been significant and consequential; you continue to be valued. Lastly, any errors in this book are mine and mine alone.

Prologue

(Part of a speech by Irene Froese at Henry & Tena Neufeld's 25th anniversary, Portage la Prairie, Manitoba, 5 July 1985. Used with permission)

There was man sent from God whose name was Henry. Now in those days Henry came from beyond the Fraser river in the guise of a social worker, and he took himself a wife from the tribe of Suderman, they did dwell in Haskett.

Recently at our Portage Mennonite Church we asked ourselves if we had any prophets in our church. And in studying the matter I came up with some marvelous observations regarding Henry. Sometime, somewhere, somehow, he was given a vision, a dream or a burden to start a Mennonite church. Where, like Abraham, he was told to go to a country he knew not.

Now the prophet Henry resembles most is Habbakuk. He is described as the great unknown. How many Henry Neufelds do you know? How many do you think there are on raspberry farms in Aldergrove? Have you ever heard of Aldergrove? Habbakuk was not a preacher, but he was a thinker and philosopher, he wrestled with God asking probing questions, and God answered.

Henry had some reservations about this prophet role, and he said: "Camel hairs and a leather girdle, that's a bit gauche, Lord, Tena's Mennonite cookbook hasn't any recipes for locusts and honey." The Lord said: "Don't despise my camel, and I have nothing against borscht."

So they journeyed, to UBC, to Ontario, to Saskatchewan, back to Manitoba, to Portage la Prairie. Now you know, all things great are bound up in things small. Tena had always wanted to leave Haskett. To where? South is the border, west is Morden, east is Altona, but north is Portage La Prairie. That seemed to be the end of the earth to this maiden from Haskett. You know, the apostle Paul always wanted to go to Rome but he never dreamt that he would get there chained to a Roman soldier.

Well Henry then began to think of building the Mennonite church, and he thought often of Ezekiel's bones coming to life. So first he tried the Mennonite Brethren church, but they kept saying "more water Henry, more water."

Then he went to the Evangelical church and they said, "no Henry, you can't ask the women what they think," and you know Henry has to know what the women think.

So he went to the Lord and he told him his problems, and the Lord said; "well, try some demonstrations, my prophet Jeremiah wept all the time," and Henry said; I'm not good at that, that isn't my style." And the Lord said: "I don't prefer that myself, there are too many long faced Mennonites around anyway. But Jeremiah, I had him walk with a yoke about his neck." Henry said: "I already have that."

Then the Lord said, "Well, Jeremiah walked 500 miles to the Euphrates to bury his girdle, and then went back to dig it up." And Henry groaned and he said, "Oh no Lord, can't you see the cartoon in the *Daily Graphic*, 'prophet Neufeld dreamed he walked 500 miles to buy his wife's 18 hour Playtex.'"

God said, "and Ezekiel, I had him do this other demonstration, he cut off all his hair, and one-third of it he burned, one-third he scattered to the wind, and one- third he chopped with a sword." And I think Henry tried this. Just last Sunday I was talking to Marlene and I said, "Have you ever noticed how Henry's beard has changed over the years, sometimes it was off, sometimes it was little, sometimes it was bigger."

So one summer the Menno Enns' and the Tony Peters' and the Neufelds spent the summer at roadside fellowships, otherwise known as campgrounds. On the last Sunday of summer the three of them were sitting like Elijah of old, discouraged under the juniper tree, and they were wondering where they would go to church next Sunday. And while they were discussing this a little black cloud came over and it came closer till it was right over them and suddenly there was a bolt of lightning and a crash of thunder. And Tony said, "oh schreck" and Menno said, "if sound travels at 1780kms /hour, that should have struck us." And Henry was speechless. He remembered Noah, and he remembered Jonah. They thought of leaving.

But another streak of lightning shot down, there was a roll of thunder and a voice said, "How long can you guys tread water?" And Tony said, "I have to ask my banker." And Menno said, "the earth's surface is 196,950,000 square miles and if it rains at the rate of 50mm a day for 40…" and Henry interrupted and said "you guys, where can we get a building for next Sunday?"

And then it came to pass that the next Sunday the Enns', the Peters,' the Neufelds, and the Froeses, whom they rescued from the Baptist waters where they had hung their harps, met for the first service of the Portage Mennonite church.

Did Henry get to work? He remembered Noah, he remembered Jonah, he worked like Jeremiah, he wrote letters to the "captives in Babylon" and his scribe typed them for him. And the captives responded….

So, it came to pass that God and Henry were having a conversation again and Henry wanted to know what happens to prophets when their jobs are done. And God said, "some went to write their memoirs." And Henry said "I've already done that, they're in the archives."

And God said, "and some of my prophets died as martyrs, and some I sent into captivity, and some went into exile. For you a ticket to Thailand, and see if you can teach them the password, Mennonite."

There was man sent from God, he went from beyond the Assiniboine with his wife to a country he knew not.

Introduction

Perhaps the most psychologically significant kind of movement that an individual can make is geographical relocation of home.
Alvin Toffler.

We all come from somewhere. The homes and places we inhabit contribute to the shaping of our lives. Every human event happens somewhere. Attachment to a place aids a person's identity by tying the locales of the past to the present. We learn to behave in a certain way in our homes, places of work, and neighbourhoods. Our transformational experiences happen in specific places. Emotional attachment to the places of our lives becomes part of our identity. Visiting our childhood homes and communities brings an adult perspective to our childhood and our past.

Seeking connections to our roots helps us understand our past. We visit the places of our past to remember and recall. Visiting places where we once lived and where our ancestors lived is part of a quest to find the genetic life patterns of our ancestors. I can envisage my father, in sub-zero Manitoba with a team of horses and a large sled sawing ice blocks in the Assiniboine River near Headingly and hauling them to Winnipeg to earn a few dollars.

There is a deep association with and to the places where we were born and grew up, where we live now, or where we have had particularly moving experiences. This association is a point of departure from which we orient ourselves in the world.

Some people stay in one place for most of their lives, others move, sometimes by choice, sometimes by necessity. For some a sense of home is forever fractured due to frequent family moves during childhood. Revolutions, war, economic opportunities, natural disasters, and other factors result in people leaving one place and adapting or trying to adapt to a new environment. Such moves often involve changes in language, customs, and work patterns. Refugees continue to face these adaptive challenges that have been present throughout history.

Today millions are relegated to temporary asylum in refugee camps with only vague hopes of returning home and uncertainty about resettling elsewhere. Anxiety about the future combined with apprehensiveness about life in a foreign land requires major adjustments. This adaptation to the new is often accompanied by nostalgia for an earlier place and memories of a good way of life. Giving a place to those who have none is a healing process, which is why the refugee resettlement work of organizations like Mennonite Central Committee is so important.

In *A Place For You* Paul Tournier addresses themes of rootlessness, belonging, attachment and displacement. The concept of "place" is a theme throughout history, beginning with Adam and Eve being dispatched from Eden: a paradise to which they could not return because armed angels guard the entrance to Eden. John Milton recognizes this loss in *Paradise Lost* when the angel assures Adam that though he may no longer reside in Eden he shall possess a happier paradise within his heart, one he can carry wherever he goes.

The patriarch Abraham is called to leave his place, the well-developed and urban civilization of Ur. He takes up a nomadic existence and sets off on a great adventure of faith. Then, to avoid a dispute about land with his nephew he leaves again for a new place. The biblical stories strongly suggest that God calls people away from a comfortable place, to begin anew. Jesus called his disciples from their comfortable zones to new challenges.

Many migrants have a nostalgic yearning for places, people and events of their past and the loss of meaningful relationships is often painful. We saw this repeatedly when working with refugees in Thailand. When asked if they'd like to return to their homeland, inevitably the answer was "yes, if it's safe to do so."

What effect did leaving Ukraine on a few hours notice have on my parents? Any major moves I've made have been planned in advance; I've not experienced the traumatic disruption of having to leave on short notice. It's hard to imagine deciding to leave and then, in a matter of hours, departing from a way of life and a place that was home to my father for the first 37 years of his life.

My parents abandoned a successful farm operation that had been in the family for generations. Except for a few hastily packed crates, they left everything. They walked away from their land and their assets and by the time their train entered Estonia their last money had been taken: they were penniless asylum seekers. The jarring statement recorded at our parent's immigration interview in Halifax describes their economic situation: *Money in possession belonging to passenger? None.*

More than abandoning assets, they left lifelong friends and a community that had educated and nurtured them. Uprooting often means separation from one's loved ones and relatives. For our mother, leaving meant she'd never see her mother again and would lose contact with her only sibling for years. Mother and her sister finally met again in 1953 when Aunt Anna, Uncle Alex and their son Rudy visited us in BC from their new Pennsylvania home. Memory of our places is important, especially for those who experience displacement; whose connections to family and country have been forcefully severed.

In a German refugee camp, en route to an unknown place, my parents experienced the death of their firstborn child, Willi. Mother treasured the one picture she had of Willi's grave, his final place. Dad said farewell to his brother, his sister, and his father and stepmother who left for Brazil; he would not see any of them again. I marvel at our parents' resilience and their remarkable capacity for adaptation. They had to let go of their past, no matter how precious it was, and move into a void, facing total uncertainty about starting over.

The quest for place is common; a destination, an Eden, is sought and yet paradise is always elusive. Eden is only a memory and return there often impossible. For some a time in the desert is required, a temporary refuge or retreat to seek a new place. By leaving one's place and starting anew one might eventually replace some of what was lost; this was the case for my parents. Canada provided freedom, the opportunity to work, right to follow their faith and provision of a safe place for their children.

In an era of technological change we need a place of inner calmness and serenity. In *Paradise Lost* the angel Michael assures Adam, on being expelled from Eden, that he'll find a "paradise happier far."

Our parents never regained the place they left in Ukraine, but with faith, hard work, and cautious optimism, they provided nurturing places for their children. The stages of our lives are unfailingly marked by the places where we and our ancestors lived. This book is arranged around the places of our lives and how those places shaped my life.

When you move to another place you must change your headman. This Hmong proverb is a reminder that when relocating we cannot take the status and prestige of our previous place with us. We start over after leaving Eden.

....

The title, "*In this Place*" is from the book of Jeremiah, chapter 7, where the prophet tells the people to do good and God will dwell with them "in this place." We are all on a journey and each place provides a challenge to do good and be blessed.

Chapter 1: Manitoba, The First Place, 1937 – 1944

Antisthenes says that in a certain faraway land the cold is so intense that words freeze as soon as they are uttered, and after some time they thaw and become audible, so that words spoken in winter go unheard until the next summer. Plutarch, Moralia.

On an icy and stormy January night Herman W. Neufeld crouched on the hood of a friend's car cleaning snow off the windshield so the driver could find his way to Winnipeg's Concordia hospital. There Sarah (nee Bartel) Neufeld gave birth to Henry – the birth certificate says Heinrich - on January 26, 1937. Presumably I was named after Dad's brother in Brazil. We lived near Pigeon Lake, Manitoba at the time.

There were three older children:
Hilda, born 21 June 1929 in Ohrloff, Ukraine
Margaret, born 26 April 1931, in Steinbach, Manitoba.
Hans (John) Herman, born 12 November 1933 at Concordia Winnipeg.

My earliest memories are of Springstein; I recall Dad working as a farm hand for John Martens. I started school there in the pre-kindergarten era; I was simply sent to school when I was old enough. I recall starting school in the middle of the year, I think it was in springtime.

In the first grade I was caught smoking. We lived near the school and went home for lunch. A lad from Winnipeg provided the cigarettes and introduced John and me to smoking during a lunch hour. Smoking was new to me and I blew into the cigarette instead of puffing on it – an innovative and possibly successful cancer fighting strategy. Despite this naivety I managed to get the smell of smoke on me, and on arriving at school a classmate accused me of smoking. I fought with him, denying any such activity. The teacher, Miss Willms, was notified and she and school principal Gerhard Lohrenz interviewed me and I tearfully confessed. The consequences followed the next day: I received the strap on my hands in front of the class for, as Miss Willms put it, "fighting and tearing a button off a boy's shirt." No mention of smoking. Mr. Lohrenz told Dad of the episode. John and I got a lecture about smoking even though Dad smoked; he said he had not started smoking till he was well into his 20s – an allegation I have come to view with some skepticism.

The other experience with smoke was mosquito related. On a hot and humid prairie evening I was sent to the dung pile behind the barn to gather dried cow dung which was burned in a tin bucket to fend off masses of mosquitoes; this was surely an innovative and environmentally friendly precursor to mosquito coils and OFF.

Rex, our German Shepherd was a great companion for John and me. A vicious bull owned by the Martens family was to be avoided at all costs. Neighbours told Mom she should not let John and me walk through the fields when the bull was anywhere nearby. Mom told them that as long as the dog was with us we were in no danger. Sadly, Rex could not accompany us to BC.

Life for our parents was not easy; a new country, a new language, and new work. Our parents had to provide for four kids and pay off their travel debts. I recall Dad talking about cutting ice blocks in the Assiniboine River near Headingly with a six foot saw and hauling it to Winnipeg on a horse drawn sled for 70 cents an hour. We were cash poor but there was always enough food and a willingness to share what we had with others. Dad worked for various farmers and also learned carpentry in Manitoba. Years later when our parents visited us in Portage la Prairie, Dad pointed out various buildings he had built, including their house in Headingly.

As a farm labourer who was earning low wages with four children and very few other assets, Dad realized the possibility of acquiring his own farmland in Manitoba was minimal. In the fall of 1944 Dad made an exploratory train trip to BC where he found opportunities for carpentry work in the Fraser Valley. We were about to leave for a new place.

Chapter 2. British Columbia, The First Time, 1944 – 1957

If you can't see the mountains, it's raining, if you can see the mountains it's going to rain.

We arrived at the Chilliwack train station on a rainy morning in January 1945. We lived with the Wall family in Greendale until Dad rented a house. Some months later we moved to a small rented acreage near the Vedder Canal on Keith Wilson Road. We attended the Sardis Mennonite church, now called Greendale Mennonite Church.

In spring 1946 Dad bought 10 acres of virgin land at 24277 – 58th Avenue in Langley Municipality. Finally, our own place. Dad lived with one of the families in this small Mennonite community while building a basic 3-bedroom home. John and I shared one (metal bunk beds), Hilda and Margaret the other bedroom. The house was substantially enlarged in 1950. The area was called Coghlan since our post office was located on Coghlan Road, now 256 Street. When that rural post office closed our address became Aldergrove.

We cleared the bush-covered land; stumps were blasted, the land was bulldozed and roots and debris were gathered and burned. We built a barn for the cow and chickens. Three or four acres of strawberries were the primary crop on this sandy soil. We had a one-cow dairy, chickens, and a few pigs. Dad milked the cow each morning, John or I milked in the evening. Our strawberries provided insufficient income and Dad continued with construction work to make ends meet. On one construction job from August to December in 1946 Dad earned $590.50.

Our closest relatives in Canada were the Aaron Enns's in Manitoba (Mrs. Enns was Dad's sister), so extended family gatherings were unknown to us. Christmas was a time of school and church programs, good food, halvah, and gifts. Gifts were sparse; one year John and I received a crokinole board that provided many hours of fun; Dad played crokinole as well as checkers with us.

Ravines, virgin forests, and creeks in the area needed exploration. We fished in the Salmon River - more a creek than a river. In fall I recall my amazement at the decaying salmon retuning to spawn and die in their birthplace. Electricity arrived in our community in the late 1940s, it was exciting when Dad bought our first small radio and we listened to cowboy music, Hockey Night in Canada, and always the news with the volume high enough for Dad to hear. I didn't realize the impact of these daily newscasts until Mr. Parnell, in a grade 8 class, asked us to name the federal cabinet ministers. I was the only one who could name most of them, having heard their names repeatedly on the radio news: education by osmosis. Our telephone arrived in the mid 1950s.

When the tree sap started running in spring, John, I, and our friends took burlap sacks and headed for the swampy areas of local ravines looking for cascara trees. With a jackknife we peeled the bark off the tree, from the base to as high as we could reach. The moist bark came off easily and we stuffed it into the sacks. At home we spread the cascara on the roof of the woodshed to dry. Then we'd break it into small pieces, bag it and sell it at the Otter Farmer's Institute. We were unaware of the medicinal effects of cascara until one of the Wiebe boys, while peeling bark, cut his finger, sucked it in pain, absorbing blood and cascara juices. Shortly thereafter he ran off and squatted. Cascara's medicinal value became obvious.

Education

On arriving in the Chilliwack area I attended the Sumas Prairie School where Miss Vera Darling divided the class into three sections, from students having difficulties to those with none. I was gradually moved to the top group.

In Aldergrove I attended the County Line Elementary School on 56th Ave, about half a mile west of County Line Road, now 264 Street. We walked or biked the two miles to school. By grade 6 a new County Line school was built near the BC Electric Rail line on 264 Street and we travelled to school by bus. School meant a hectic schedule for Mom. Due to rapid population growth John and Margaret's high school operated in shifts; John attended early morning to noon, Margaret in the afternoon, and I was on regular school hours. Mom commented that she had kids coming and going at all hours.

In Manitoba we came home from school for lunch; in BC we took our lunch to school. Margaret recalls us complaining about the lunches Mom made for us, so Mom set out the food in the morning and told us to make our own lunches. One of my favourites was cottage cheese and syrup sandwiches; homemade cottage cheese was dryer than that in today's supermarket. Even though they were soggy by noon, they were delicious. I still enjoy Rogers Golden Syrup on cottage cheese; few try this delicacy and no one asks for the recipe.

Sometimes Mom would make us a full meat and potatoes breakfast and I would not take any lunch, relying on a major snack when I got home after school. One day the principal noticed I didn't have any lunch and summoned me to his office and asked me about it. I told him I had a big breakfast and he wanted to know exactly what I had eaten. My explanation must have satisfied him since he never asked me again.

I entered grade 7 in the newly built Langley Junior Senior High School, still located on 56 Street. I travelled by school bus and completed grade 10 there. In grade 9 our English teacher, Mr. Sherriff, had us write a one-page essay each week. A week later he read the best one to the class – after reading mine he said, "why don't you write like that every week?" That might have been the start of an interest in writing; in later years I wrote articles for several Mennonite magazines. Where does an interest in writing come from? Is it passed down from generation to generation? Dad kept a diary and looked after church subscriptions to the German language paper, *Der Bote*; I was on the board of *Canadian Mennonite*; and Bev and Andrew have had books published.

Grades 11 – 13 were spent at the Mennonite Educational Institute in Clearbrook. John had just completed his final two years of high school there and I decided to enroll there as well. A group of us travelled to the MEI with Peter Neudorf, we sat on benches in his enclosed Mercury pick-up truck. Tuition was about $150.00 per school year. Our parents encouraged us to get an education but could not afford to help financially. We earned tuition money by working at various summer jobs; strawberry fields, the peat bog in Delta, and BC Packers fish cannery in Steveston.

I graduated from MEI's grade in 1956, failing two subjects (math & physics) that I later recovered at university. Grade 13 was the equivalent of first year of university.

In the summer of 1955 I worked at a small logging firm owned by Jake Berg near Lac La Hache, B.C., driving a bull-dozer hauling logs to the mill. The other fellows were all from Manitoba and I learned some Low German that summer. At home we spoke the more formal High German, though our parents spoke Low German with each other and with friends.

One morning I was driving our family truck to school to write a Christmas exam when I blacked out and found myself crashing into a ditch. The windshield glass shattered, cutting the tendon on the large knuckle on the index finger of my left hand and cutting my jaw. I walked to a nearby home and Mr.

Eric Flowerdew took me to the Langley hospital where I was stitched up, had a cast on my left hand, and was released. Not one to faint or fall asleep while driving, I'm not sure why I blacked out.

The family farm was sold in 1959 and Dad built their retirement home at 24752 56 Avenue, Langley, and there, thanks to Canada's pension plan, they were able to live in modest comfort and enjoy their well gardened place.

Church
My initial experience of God was born in an ethnic, religious and familial context that had no lines of distinction. I was a Mennonite, as was the food I ate, the church I attended... and the family I was born into. John Goossen.

We always attended church and I recall our parents reading Scripture before breakfast and kneeling in prayer prior to retiring for the night. As a child I said a nightly prayer while standing beside Mom and then giving each parent a kiss. I can still sense Dad's musty, smoky mustache and stubbled beard.

Regular church attendance was important and all four of us were baptized in the Bethel Mennonite Church on 56[Th] Ave. I was part of a group baptized in 1954 by Rev. Johannes Regier. Baptism was held annually on Pentecost and was preceded by several months of weekly catechism instructions in the basics of the Christian faith. Young people's church activities and Friday night choir practices were our primary social outlets; the singing was secondary. My friends Peter Neudorf, Jake Friesen and I played a lot of chess.

Our church and the MEI emphasized a personal conversion experience, periodic pressurized evangelism, and a life of piety. In addition to weekly lunchtime Bible study sessions, all students assembled for a testimony meeting during the last school hour each week. A teacher had a brief sermon, after which students were expected to speak about their faith, or ask for forgiveness. "If in any way I have offended anyone I want to ask for forgiveness" was a generic refrain. Evangelistic services were held regularly in school and churches. Guilt induction was the strategy of evangelists; sometimes it was successful. Church, school and home reinforced conformity resulting in suspicion of outsiders. "Outsiders" included people of other faiths as well as non-German speaking people. There was an ethnic insularity in our Mennonite community. Our proximity to the English speaking majority - most of my classmates in elementary and junior high were non-Mennonites - the subtle message was that other religious groups didn't measure up. This attitude of religious superiority – pride - was not identified or addressed.

Our Community Crusade

Henry Neufeld, 1979. (printed in The Mennonite, *23 October 1979.)*

We arrive late and the two ushers glance at each other, silently competing to see who will get to show us in. Our usher is one of the few people we don't recognize; perhaps he thinks we're part of the "uncommitted" group here tonight. The chairs are cold and hard.

A well scrubbed and neatly dressed family walks in... they could easily do a Maytag commercial... I wonder if he's a clergyman; there's something about the way he struts in ahead of his family... that's it... he wants to see – and be seen.

Is it true that evangelicals have a contest going to see who can carry the largest Bible? I worry about hernias and lower back pain.

The preliminaries are finally over; we've sung our prescribed quota of hymns, we've dropped our coins noisily into the Colonel Sanders offering buckets... not even a whiff of fried chicken. The evangelist is forceful and clear; he's obviously a skilled orator. A freight train roars by... farmers and golfers will be out on their fields tonight... the green on number five will be coming in well now after the rain.

The chairs get harder… kids get restless… a not so old man tries half successfully to suppress a yawn... a young lad starts picking his nose… an airplane momentarily drowns out the speaker. "Salvation is a gift, free for anyone to accept," he says, a message clear for all to understand. As he raises his voice a few nodding heads jerk back to their usual position… "you can't keep your faith to yourself," he admonishes. A farmhand sleeps – soundly – his head no longer bobs up and down.

This has got to be spectator Christianity at its best. We've hired this guy to come and preach the gospel to our community's unsaved… and who crowds in here every night? Church people. The faithful. They flock here by the hundreds. How many times do they need to hear the salvation message?

Two people check their watches… he's been speaking for 35 minutes now but it doesn't seem that long. One man slowly pages through the hymnbook … a teenager picks mud – piece by piece – out of her runners… a nine year old almost twists her Dad's arm off trying to get his wristwatch into a readable position.

My daughter instructs me to inquire of her mother whether there might be gum in the bottomless purse… a high school girl wraps her fine gold necklace around her finger – again and again – slowly hypnotizing herself … and me… my daughter asks if the gum has been found yet.

Is anyone listening to the evangelist? A teenager keeps pulling her skirt down over her knees, she would have been more comfortable in denim… two kids whisper and the one closest to Dad gets an elbow in the ribs… another girl takes a handful of hair and pulls it away slowly, one strand at a time, carefully examining each one… does she have split ends? The bottomless purse finally produces, not gum but a Certs, and a silent thanks is mouthed in Mom's direction.

A clergyman in the crowd restlessly and too vigorously swings his foot back and forth, loudly proclaiming his boredom… finally he gets up and leaves the building. An elderly fellow dozes, a youth *yawns but the message is proclaimed. The evangelist does not apply any pressure, neither does he send us on a guilt trip… he must be a rare one.*

My mind wanders… it's hard to concentrate on a message I've heard 100 times before…. We don't keep teaching college students the alphabet… yet Christians come here night after night to hear the conversion message… maybe we're all kindergarten Christians who want to keep relearning the alphabet.

Quiet prayer… if we want to accept Christ or rededicate our lives then we are to fill out the form the usher gave us when we arrived. If I complete mine, will he then ask me to come forward? Once years ago, in response to an evangelists pressure to "just slip up your hand," I did and a minute later he asked those of us who had raised our hands to come forward… I felt tricked and betrayed… why can't evangelists be honest and tell us exactly how they are going to handle the altar call… why try to wring commitments out of people?

As I feared, we pause between each of the six verses of the closing hymn and those who raised their hands are asked to come forward… as a public declaration…. If we were honest we'd all be up front, but only a few move forward… how often can Christians publicly rededicate themselves before it becomes mockery?

A stone rolls noisily down the tin roof, rudely interrupting the altar call…. Most people don't need the salvation message… they need a rude interruption in their placid Christianity. Where will they learn how to examine and measure their Christian growth? Where will they learn to agonize over the pain of change that comes with growth? Where will they learn to struggle with fellow Christians, to share of themselves, to affirm each other in growth? There must be more to the Christian faith than relearning the alphabet.

Chapter 3. Maryland and Ontario: 1957 –1959

The twenties are tryout years and what motivates young people are two contradictory impulses. The urge to create a structure that will serve their needs into the (barely) foreseeable future and the fear of being locked into a life pattern that will ultimately prove unsatisfying or limited. Jane Adams.

In fall 1956, after grade 13, I worked at Canada Packers in Vancouver ($1.37 per hour) living with my sister Hilda and John Warkentin. I was laid off at Christmas and in January 1957 began working for contractor Walter Goertz, building the Bethel Mennonite Church on 56 Ave, Aldergrove, ($1.60 per hour).

Brother John attended Canadian Mennonite Bible College in Winnipeg and I felt some pressure to do the same, but didn't want to follow his pattern. Unclear about my future and not wanting to continue in construction, I applied to Mennonite Central Committee (MCC) in Akron, Pennsylvania for a voluntary service position. I left for Akron, Pennsylvania in July 1957.

Leaving home is a loosening of child-parent ties and represents a desire to distance oneself from parents and become independent, to find one's place in life. My sisters left home: they went to Vancouver to work. John went to Winnipeg to study, and I must have wanted to get far away from it all: I went to Maryland and Ontario. The paths my siblings and I took accomplished the same goal: leaving the parental home to establish independence and identity.

Maryland

MCC placed me with a group of 15 volunteers at the National Institutes of Health (NIH), in Bethesda, Maryland for the summer. We were human guinea pigs and in return MCC was paid by NIH for each volunteer; MCC used the funds to help pay for other programs. The volunteers received $10.00 per month from MCC. This program was discontinued in 1975, around the time that the US military draft was abolished and alternatives to military service were no longer needed.

We were "normal control patients," involved in mental health research. We received excellent medical care and were assessed by doctors, psychologists and psychiatrists. We were subjected to a variety of medical tests, drugs and experiments; most memorable was a 72-hour sleep deprivation test from Sunday morning to Wednesday morning. During this time we were under constant supervision by nurses and attendants and were tested for response to stimuli. The four of us played pool, chess (I beat one of the psychiatrists), did crafts, and went for walks at all hours of the night. On returning from one of those walks, I sleepwalked into a door; no damage to the door or me, but I woke up. During the last eight hours we noticed that our thinking was affected – we couldn't recall the names of others in our group.

At NIH we had a lot of free time; we toured Washington DC and we got passes to Washington Capitals baseball games where we watched Boston's Ted Williams and also notable Yankees - Mickey Mantle, Joe Dimaggio - and others of that era. On Saturday nights we'd go to the Potomac River for free concerts on a floating stage called Watergate; which later became the site of the Watergate Hotel, famous for toppling President Nixon.

One Sunday morning a few of us were trying to decide which church to attend and I suggested a Methodist church within walking distance. Charles Johnson, a black fellow, said he'd not be able to attend there. Being Canadian, young, and naïve, I asked why. He politely explained that blacks were not admitted to that church. We attended elsewhere and I began to learn about racism.

One of the benefits of the NIH experience was interacting with caring professional people who were not necessarily Christian. Growing up with skepticism of non – Mennonites, I was pleasantly surprised that these people were genuinely interested in me, and were not critical or disdainful of my naiveté or my faith. At the end of the summer one doctor came to see my roommate and me; he had reviewed our file and said we were both quite capable of handling college work. He encouraged us to pursue further education. With only average high school marks, this was an affirming nudge I needed.

Ontario
"It's an extra dividend when you like the girl you're in love with."
Clark Gable.

In mid-September 1957 our unit at NIH disbanded and I went to MCC headquarters (Akron, Pennsylvannia) for orientation. A pleasant surprise was to meet my Manitoba cousin Aaron Enns there. Aaron and Esther Shantz met in Akron, married and became good friends. Staying in the US meant eligibility for the US military draft, so to avoid that MCC placed me at Ailsa Craig Boys Farm near London, Ontario (now Craigwood) a home for about 20 boys. My job description was building maintenance, but much time was spent supervising boys, especially recreational activities on weekends and evenings. Intrigued with the boys' behaviour, I began thinking about social work as a career. Delmar and Alice Rempel worked there for a few months; another friendship that continued for years.

Football, basketball, and floor hockey injuries led to knee surgery at London's St. Joseph's hospital in November 1958. I had a cast from hip to ankle for a month. My parents and Margaret sent me train fare to go home to BC for Christmas. I noticed changes; some of my former friends were away, others were married, and I felt I didn't belong in that place anymore. In 18 months away from home, their lives took a certain direction, mine another. The place was different and so was I.

On a warm July evening in 1958 I walked through the Boys Farm kitchen and noticed a strikingly beautiful blonde at the counter eating a bowl of cereal. I introduced myself, we talked briefly and I walked out and sat down on the patio steps beside Lynn, one of the boys. Lynn commented on the nice looking new cook. I readily agreed. Tena Suderman had arrived.

My roommate and I agreed on Tena's beauty and I told him he had two weeks to pursue her since my sister Margaret was arriving from BC and she and I would spend some time visiting relatives in Ontario. Fortunately Dave was unsuccessful with Tena so she and I began spending time together. Ted and Alice Peters from Nebraska kindly let us use their car. I appreciated Tena's beauty and pleasantness, we conversed easily, we could both tolerate silence, and she was fun to be with. And, since she was a cook I got to eat her food. On my birthday Tena made baked Alaska, a tradition she continued for many years.

In May 1959 Tena and I accompanied Hugo and Eldora Hildebrand on a trip to Ottawa to visit the Ottawa Children's Village. Hugo let us use his car that evening and at a park somewhere along the Ottawa River, Tena readily agreed to marry me. I was ecstatic. Our $10.00 a month income did not allow me to buy a ring, that came at Christmas. We agreed to work for a year, get married and then I'd attend university. In July 1959 Tena and I left Ontario for Manitoba by train. I spent some time at the Suderman home near Haskett, met many of Tena's family and took the train to B.C. where my parents met me at the Mission railway station.

Chapter 4. B.C. The Second Time: 1959 – 1965

Drove to our original farm... the property has been sold to a developer and the home is being demolished. I walked through the house and on a partly demolished kitchen wall found the original building permit from 1950 - value of project: $1,000.00. (Diary, July 14, 1976.)

My parents sold their 10-acre farm in 1959 and Dad built their retirement home on 56 St. near the Bethel Mennonite Church. I helped Dad for a week or so in July 1959, then Peter Neudorf and I began work for Columbia Bitulithic near Revelstoke, B.C. on construction of the Roger's Pass highway ($1.70 per hour). Waldemar Janzen from our community was our boss. Peter bought a tent, I bought a camp stove and we lived in the gravel pit and worked on deafeningly noisy rock crusher, about 6 miles east of Revelstoke. No noise protection for our ears, which likely contributed to my hearing loss in later years. By mid-November it was too cold to work and I began work at Canada Packers in Vancouver. Just before Christmas I flew to Manitoba (my first airplane ride) to spend Christmas with Tena and present her with an engagement ring, which I could now afford. After a week there I went to Boissevain to visit John and Hilda Warkentin on their farm, and took the train from Brandon back to B.C.

Brother John and Anne Neufeld left for Uruguay in spring 1960 so I had use of their car. In early July I left for Manitoba and our wedding. My parents left earlier to visit Mom's sister, the Sartzchenkos, in Pennsylvania and came to our wedding on their way home.

After our wedding in Winkler, Manitoba and honeymoon in Devils Lake and Bottineau, North Dakota, we left for BC. We stayed with my parents for a few days and then rented a suite at 1126 West 11th Ave. in Vancouver for $75.00 per month, our first place. Tena worked at the Vancouver General Hospital, a short distance from our home. On September 19, 1960 Tena had her appendix removed at the Chatham House Hospital on 14th Ave.

In Vancouver we attended the Vancouver Mennonite Mission Church (later renamed as Mountainview Mennonite Church) and enjoyed the "young adults" events.

University of BC (1960 – 65)

That is what learning is. You suddenly understand something you've understood all your life, but in a new way. Doris Lessing. *Very soon after graduation I … found myself intellectually bankrupt. In other words I was what is called a distinguished graduate.* Stephen Leacock

I enrolled at the University of B.C. in September 1960. I enjoyed undergraduate studies, majoring in English and Psychology. Tena typed my essays. My most memorable course was a course on John Milton with Prof. Roy Daniells. In his first class he told us we should borrow our grandmother's Bible and start reading it; studying Milton required a knowledge of Scripture. A renowned scholar of Milton, he knew much of the Bible from memory, having grown up in a strict Plymouth Brethren family. Daniells was a powerful orator, a dramatic reader, and an intense and gentle professor. I recall his dramatic reading of the ending of *Samson Agonistes*, then, with tears streaming down his cheeks, he walked out of the classroom. We just sat there.

The only university text I still have is from this course on John Milton.

Money was scarce; I did janitor work in the engineering building every Monday evening for $1.75 per hour, a job I had for three years. In May 1961 we moved to 1075 West Broadway where we were caretakers in a six-suite apartment block; our monthly rent was reduced to $50.00 because of our caretaking duties. The most onerous task was lighting the ancient furnace/water heater three times a day. In summer 1961 I worked at the Pacific National Exhibition for a few weeks, then at Canada Packers and the BC Packers fish cannery in Steveston.

Andrew was born on July 9, 1961 at Vancouver's Salvation Army's Grace Hospital. At that time fathers were not allowed in the delivery room and a nurse brought newborn Andrew to me. I was amazed at the beauty of each of our newborns: perfectly clear skin and peaceful sleep.

With Tena at home caring for Andrew our financial situation was precarious. John & Anne Neufeld returned from Uruguay in September 1961. We returned their VW and relied on public transit. During Christmas holidays I worked at the post office. Tena sold Avon products. There were no extra funds, but we got by.

In summer 1962 I worked as a guard at Oakalla prison farm ($13.50 per day) on Royal Oak Avenue in Burnaby, a provincial prison for offenders sentenced to less than two years. We had no training I was told to show up on Saturday morning. A guard brought out eight inmates, gave me a ring of keys and told me to take the inmates to the garage.
"Where's the garage?" I asked. "Just follow the inmates," the guard said.
We got to the garage and the inmates said:
"Unlock the door, we need to get the keys for the vehicles."
I was dumbfounded. This was a jail, these were prisoners, and they wanted keys for vehicles: I was perplexed and refused.

The prisoners started taking out a window to gain entrance and I decided I might as well open the garage door. Once inside they pointed to a small locked office and said:

"Open that door, we need the keys for the trucks."

I refused and this time they had no way of getting in. I saw a telephone, asked an inmate what building we came from, I phoned "Westgate A" and was told another guard would be there soon. He arrived shortly, explaining that he saw us walk by and assumed I was one of the regular guards. He opened the office door, the prisoners got their keys and were soon gone to their jobs. I commented to the guard that this was a stressful introduction to my job. He assured me I had done fine, the inmates learned that they couldn't get anything they wanted from me. It was a frightening and anxiety producing introduction to the job.

Mostly I worked mostly from 4:00 – 11:00 p.m. on a tier with 22 inmates. Again, no training. The inmates sat around talking, reading, or playing games. Apprehensive and scared, I didn't know what to do or what my job was. I anxiously paced up and down the tier. One inmate said: "Shaking it rough, eh?" I asked him to repeat and still didn't understand what he meant. Later I learned that new inmates pace a lot; they haven't settled into the prison routine. In prison lingo "they're doing rough time" or "shaking it rough." I realized that the adjustment for new guards was no different than for new prisoners. In a few days I settled into the routine and my pacing stopped. I discovered I could learn more about prison life and rules by from the prisoners than from other guards.

A fall 1962 advertisement in the UBC student newspaper the *Ubyssey* read:

Responsible couple wanted. Free board and room for both plus $100.00 a month pay in exchange for wife to do the following duties:

1.Look after two children (age 3, 5); 2. cook and organize meals; 3. lighthouse keeping work and look after children's needs.

Spacious West Van home. Car desirable. Reasonable time off, employer university student. Phone: WA 2-4380. Ask for Helen.

We phoned Helen Burns and arranged to meet in her British Properties home in West Vancouver. She phoned a few days later and asked us to come live with her. We bought a used Volkswagon from Plimley's for $300.00. Since we had no money, brother-in-law Jake Bergen kindly co-signed a bank loan for us and we had our first car. We moved to Helen's at 1010 Eyremont Drive, on October 31,1962. In addition to our room and board, Tena received a small salary.

Tena looked after Andrew as well as Helen's two kids, Grant and Brenda. Helen and I attended UBC, sometimes traveling together. Helen moved to Hawaii in spring and allowed us to stay in the house, using her credit card for groceries until mid-May. One of Helen's extended family members wanted to move into the house, so we agreed to move into a pent-house apartment the family owned in West Vancouver at 1845 Bellevue Ave, where we celebrated my BA graduation with my parents, Dad appreciated the champagne. Mom said Dad bought a *Vancouver Sun* the day UBC graduates were listed to find my name there.

We bought Helen's Singer sewing machine, TV, and a Hallicrafter radio all for $100.00. With Helen away some of her relatives felt we would steal her things and complained to Helen. Helen wrote her relatives a letter:

"I also heard that you were worried that Tina and Henry were absconding with some of my things. To set your mind at rest, first, let me tell you something about Tina and Henry. One, they are the most honest two people that I've ever met, two they are Menenites, and true to their religion. If they took anything that I didn't give them it would bother them the rest of their life. To set your mind at rest... I shall try to make a list of things I gave Henry & Tina. ... If they seem to be departing with a lot of things, don't worry about it... as I say a lot of it is their own in the first place... and the rest be reassured is what I gave them." (Letter from Helen Burns to her relatives, spring 1963)

Helen wrote us:

From what I gather from Tony you may be having problems... I only hope they are short lived. First let me say, I KNOW THAT NEITHER OF YOU WOULD TAKE A THING THAT I HADN'T GIVEN YOU, OR THAT WASN'T YOURS. And I truly mean that—I trust you two far above most members of my family.

On June 1, 1963 we moved to a small 2nd floor apartment at 7892 Heather Street; a marked contrast to the British Properties penthouse living: instead of mountains and water, we now saw industrial areas and sawmills along the Fraser river.

In summer I sold Fuller brushes in Vancouver's west end. Not an enjoyable job but I earned a few dollars. Wendy was born on July 10, 1963 at Vancouver's Grace Hospital, our first daughter. Tena had some bleeding after Wendy's birth and returned to the hospital for a D&C.

With two children and limited funds, I applied for scholarships. I was awarded a $1500.00 bursary from the BC government for one year of social work studies. About a week later we received a telegram from Saskatchewan offering me a 2-year bursary at $300.00 per month plus tuition fees. I burst into tears of joy and relief at this good news and we readily accepted this answer to prayer. A condition of this bursary was that I work in Saskatchewan for at least three years. Saskatchewan did not have a school of social work and offered bursaries to get social workers.

My studies in social work began in fall 1963. I recall Prof. Adrian Marriage doing a lecture on the similarity between social work and Chinese brain washing. For two days a week I had a field placement in the public welfare office in Haney (Maple Ridge). In April 1964 we moved to a two bedroom home owned by Vern Dillabough at 12553 – 14th Ave, Haney. I worked at the local public welfare office throughout the summer.

On 5 September 1964 we moved to 6282 Main Street ($125.00 rent per month) and I entered my final year of social work studies. My two-day a week field placement at the Burnaby Mental Health Centre focused on disturbed children and their families. Working with psychologists and psychiatrists was an excellent learning experience.

Social work studies culminated with a one-hour oral exam with three professors. It was a tense time because one could lose the entire year by failing this exam. Mine was scheduled for 9:00 a.m. and fortunately I didn't know till later that the same panel of professors had failed the fellow before me. I was relieved when one of the professors came out to congratulate me.

This marked the ends of five years at UBC, the first three were most difficult financially and at one point I seriously considered leaving university. We knew that if we could get through these years it would be worthwhile. There was no money for holidays – walks, picnics in Stanley Park was our recreation. We were in a survival mode and did not have time to be involved in the emerging hippie movement. We left university with only a few hundred dollars of student loan debt.

Tena was a careful manager of our meager household funds. She's always been a shrewd planner and budgeter, a bargain hunter, and thrifty. In later years, if we ate out, she often commented "I could have made a make a better meal for much less than this cost us." Her adeptness at managing finances meant that we have had virtually no disagreements about money.

Chapter 5. Saskatchewan, The Only Time: 1965 – 1968

Saskatchewan is much like Texas - except it's more friendly to the United States. Adlai Stevenson

On 5 May 1965 we left for Saskatoon; leaving the lush west coast in early May and arriving in dry, barren, and windy Saskatchewan was a bit of a shock. We were fortunate to be assigned to Saskatoon rather than a more remote area. Saskatoon is a beautiful city with a winding river and lots of trees.

We rented a small two-bedroom house at 1118 – 13th St. E for $90.00 per month. I had a caseload of physically and mentally disabled people; the objective was to get them into the work-force. Salary: $468.00 per month. After one year I was pro-moted to a supervisory position in Saskatoon. In retrospect it was a premature posting; a few more years of experience as a caseworker would have been desirable. However there were few people with MSW degrees and the assumption was that we were competent.

Except for Delmar and Alice Rempel, whom I knew from working at Ailsa Craig, we knew no one in Saskatoon. In deciding on a Mennonite church to attend I developed a simple rating scale and we evaluated each church after a Sunday service. Some pastors came to visit us and when I mentioned the rating scale idea they seemed threatened that anyone would evaluate them and their churches. One pastor asked how we'd feel if there was a rating scale for church members, and I shocked him by saying it was a good idea. We decided on Nutana Park Mennonite Church, nearest to our home and where Delmar and Alice attended. I was youth leader there.

We were not accustomed to prairie life; we drove to the edge of town to watch springtime dust storms, or went for a ride in the country by picking a road, driving for half an hour, and turning around and retuning home. We bought a barbecue and stayed around home. Saskatoon is a beautiful city with a winding river and lots of trees. Winters were severe and our VW had difficulty surviving and was replaced by a more durable Ford. It was a one-day drive to Tena's family in Manitoba and we made that trip a number of times.

During the Prince Albert winter festival we visited friends and watched some of the events standing on the river ice in −50F weather.

Bev was born in Saskatoon on 26 December 1967. There were some serious complications after the birth; Tena had *placenta acreta* (a 1 in 10,000 condition) where the placenta attaches itself to the wall of the uterus rather than being expelled. This condition was present after Wendy's birth, but was not diagnosed at the time. Fortunately we were in a city where a gynecologist was available - otherwise Tena would likely not have survived. Her recovery was slow but consistent; we had help looking after the children from a couple from Tonga who lived nearby.

We felt somewhat isolated in Saskatoon. My three-year obligation to work in Saskatchewan ended in May 1968 and we began looking for work opportunities elsewhere.

The 60's, with issues like student activism, drugs, hippies, and the Vietnam war did not affect us much. Aware of them, we were preoccupied with our young children, completing my education, and getting established in the work world.

Chapter 6. Manitoba, The Second Time: 1968 –1985

I once drove back through southern Manitoba at night. I was stunned by the beauty the prairies can offer. I remember the sleepy farming towns at rest - a reminder of the legacy of honest, hard working people who built a nation. Duane W. Berke

In spring 1968 I was offered a supervisory job at the Children's Aid Society in Portage La Prairie Manitoba. ($900.00 per month.) The location was appealing because it was an hour's drive from Winnipeg and a bit further to Tena's parent's farm south of Winkler. We also felt a small city (15,000) was preferable to a larger urban area for raising a family.

In late July 1968 we moved to 318 Crescent Road, Portage La Prairie, (monthly rent: $175.00) a beautiful location on Crescent Lake and within walking distance to my office and two blocks from Prince Charles School where Andrew and Wendy attended.

Stanley Harper, an aboriginal student from Island Lake, Manitoba, lived with us for about a year, attending a local high school. One day at supper Wendy said:
"Dad, is Stanley an Indian?" Fortunately I had my mouth full and before I could reply Andrew said:
"No, he isn't."
"Yes, he is," retorted Wendy.
"No, he isn't."

"Yes, he is."

"Well, Dad, is he?" Wendy asked.

"Why don't you ask him?" I said.

"Stanley, are you an Indian?" Wendy asked without hesitation.

"Yes," replied a smiling Stanley.

"See, I told you," said Wendy to Andrew.

Stanley joined us in hearty laughter.

In July 1970 we bought a house built in the late 1800's at 54 –5th Street SE in Portage, for $17,500. It was across the street from Victoria school where our children completed their elementary school and only two blocks from my office at the Children's Aid Society. A large four-bedroom home, it had two stairways that the kids enjoyed. This is the home where they'll have most of their childhood memories. The kids and I came home for lunch; Tena creatively came up with meals for all of us. A working class area, we had some colourful neighbours.

Our friend Harvey Sawatzky and I decided to venture into real estate and we bought and sold number of houses. It was a pleasure working with Harvey; I regretted leaving Harvey to look after this business when we left Manitoba.

Family vacations consisted of regular trips to BC to visit my parents, with a stop in Saskatoon. Sometimes in winter we'd go south – to Grand Forks, North Dakota - for a weekend in a hotel with a pool.

Work

One of the symptoms of an approaching nervous breakdown is the belief that one's work is terribly important. Bertrand Russell

About a year after joining the Children's Aid Society we had some personnel problems in the Winkler and Morden area. In light of the Mennonite population there and my knowledge of Low German I offered to work there, spending a few days each week in that area. I still have letters from some seriously depressed people with whom I worked. It was also my intro-duction to child abuse in the Mennonite community. After a year or so I turned the caseload over to another social worker.

I had responsibility for the adoption staff; we placed infants as well older children in adoptive homes. The older children were often placed in other provinces and in the USA. We believed it was better for these kids to have permanent homes rather than grow up in foster care. We developed an approach to processing adoptive applicants in groups rather than indi-vidual couples. This proved quite successful and became the model used by other agencies. I did presentations on this process at several national child welfare conferences.

Fellow social worker Joe Scaletta and I decided to do some fee for service counseling. Working in an agency our salary is assured and we wanted to see if people would pay us for our counseling skills. Several doctors and lawyers in town referred clients to us; we saw people in the evenings, usually using doctors' offices. Generally our clients were happy with our services and willingly paid us. When Joe moved to BC I continued with some private counseling.

Our CAS management team consisted of Bruce Fraser, Executive Director, and three supervisors: John Chudzik, Lloyd Metcalfe and me. To facilitate working together as a management team we had help from a consultant at Quetico Centre east of Atikokan, Ontario. Initially we worked at iden-tifying our individual styles of organizational behaviour. The idea was to learn to function with a maximum concern for people and an equal concern for productivity; this was seen as the ideal in organizational behaviour.

We found that our attempts to become the ideal organization didn't materialize and we realized that what we needed was a series of ideal strategies that would guide the organization, rather than a specific blueprint or model. Instead of focusing on an ideal, we moved to a system of strength management. This approach assumed that people don't change much and that most of us have gotten to where we are due to our past successes. What we've done has worked for us and rather than trying to change our behaviour into something "ideal," we need to develop the skills we already have. This involved identifying individual behavioural strengths and weaknesses and getting colleagues to help us when we're in areas of weakness.

In 1975 I was asked to join Professor Joe Ryant from the University of Manitoba School of Social Work and four others in an eight-month review of child welfare services in Manitoba. This involved traveling to Winnipeg and other areas of Manitoba. The Ryant Report, our final product has gathered a lot of dust. For me it was a valuable experience in assessing services and identifying needs.

In 1977 Executive Director Bruce Fraser left the agency and I declined the invitation to apply for his position. I was the staff representative on the CAS Board committee interviewing candidates for the position. Jim Dubray was hired in 1977 and thus began an era of turmoil. Jim was more authoritarian in his management style; creating a marked shift in the organization culture. A number of staff left the agency. I didn't want to leave because our children wanted to complete high school in Portage; our family was more important than my work. I found it difficult to work as part of the management group and when our adoption worker left I applied for that position. Jim granted my wish because he said he didn't want me to leave the agency. I became a social worker again.

Long discussion with Executive Director Jim today re trust – he's got a problem of not being able to trust me and basis this on suspicions and presumptions. Was disappointed and hurt by his approach. (Diary, February 2, 1979)

Unfortunately the organizational pathology has not yet run its course. (Diary, June 9, 1981)

The turmoil continued; Jim fired several people, and social workers unionized. Three of us opposed unionization, and I presented a statement on our behalf to the Labour Relations Board. Our argument was that unionization would not solve the agency's problems. Unionization proceeded; I kept my head down and did my job.

With staff changes things settled down and I returned to a supervisory position after a few years. I pioneered the reunion of adult adoptees with their birth parents. These cases required investigative work to locate the birth parents. Our records were at least 20 years old; we had no current information about the birth parents. There was a the risk of upsetting the birth mother's current marriage if the birth mother had not told her spouse about the child she had placed for adoption many years earlier.

In the first adoptee/birth parent reunion I worked on, I located the birth mother in another province. With her original name in the phone book I assumed she was single. I phoned her, identified myself and asked if she had any idea why I was calling. Without hesitation she said: "It's about the child I gave up for adoption 23 years ago." I almost fell off my chair. In our conversation she mentioned her husband. I said I assumed she was single because I found her name in the phone book. "I left it in there so you could find me," she said. Again my chair risked losing me. The birth mother and daughter agreed to correspond and after some months the mother and daughter met in Manitoba. I met with each of them prior to their meeting, preparing them for what might happen. It was the first of many remarkable reunions; each one a unique story.

Jim Dubray resigned as Executive Director in September 1984 and I was appointed Interim Executive director. Although invited again to apply for the Executive Director's position, I declined. There was a time when I wanted that position; not so any more. That fall Tena and I drove to Ontario and Wisconsin and had long discussions about our future. Staying at the agency with a new Executive Director could be awkward. I was one of the longest serving staff and colleagues might consult me rather than the new Director. This could create an awkward situation for both of us. Also, Bev, our youngest, was in grade 12 and our commitment to stay in Portage till the children finished school was soon expiring. It was time to consider options.

I was the staff representative on the selection committee for a new Executive Director; Dennis Schellenberg was hired. Dennis and Linda bought our house at 54 - 5th street S.E. We bought a newer Cape Cod style home, at 407 Dufferin Avenue West in Portage, moving there in early April 1985. We thought a newer home would provide fewer maintenance problems if we were away for a few years.

I wanted an occupational change and three options emerged: a social work job elsewhere, further education, or an entirely different line of work. I wasn't that keen on more social work, and the prospect of several years of study was not appealing. That left the option of a different type of work. Over the years Tena had periodically said that we should do more MCC work, and in 1984 we applied for a position with MCC.

My diary entry has some prophetic words:
My last day of work at CAS. After 17 years at the same job it's hard to imagine leaving, even though I have a three-year leave of absence, I somehow doubt if I'll ever be back here to work again. (Diary, June 28, 2005)

Management team colleagues (1971)

One of our management team building activities at the Children's Aid Society included hearing how other team members perceived each of us. Here's what they said about me at a management retreat at Quetico Centre, Atikokan.

He is decisive, sound and creative but often settles for work-able solutions.
He has strong convictions which he will stand up for intensely but he will also accept compromises. When conflict arises <u>outside</u>

of himself he tries to identify the reasons for it and/or get an equitable solution. When directly involved and self-confident he will try to win his position; when threatened he avoids or withdraws. Under tension he feels unsure which way to turn or shift to avoid further pressure. Once sorted out, he handles his emotions with confidence.

Uses humour extensively to shift attention away from the serious side, to give perspective, and to sell himself. He seeks to maintain a good steady pace, when the situation demands he exerts rigorous effort. He rarely leads in "boss-risk" situations, but supports. He needs to identify and risk self in confrontation. He needs to exercise leadership ability more often. Needs to express convictions more objectively, think about it for a few minutes, consider the other side, timing.

Final evaluation, Children's Aid Society of Central Manitoba, 1985

As Interim Executive Director there is clear consensus that he functioned at a very high level… there were a number of fairly sensitive and controversial case decisions that had to be made… Henry has the unique ability to focus on goals and end results there is no doubt he has been a major stabilizing force in the organization in terms of conflict resolution and personal reconciliations.

Children

"People who like to read tend to do a lot better in life than those who don't."
Scott Peck.

Tena and I are both avid readers; reading to our kids when they were small was common. Tena regularly took the children to the local library. Andrew's grade 1 teacher in Saskatoon said she'd do many things in school, but primarily she wanted to get the kids to read. "If they can read everything else is available to them," she said. Our kids are keen readers and bibliophiles.

All three took piano lessons, initially during the lunch hour from Mrs. Eveline Cox, then from Mrs. Erickson, lastly from Harvey and Margaret Sawatzky. We bought our piano from J.J. McLean in Winnipeg in 1970 for $300.00 and 30 years later donated it to camp Squeah near Hope, BC. Wendy was most gifted in piano; Bev played the trombone at school. Andrew was not particularly musically interested.

Andrew played some baseball as a youngster, but was more interested in golf. At age 5 or 6 years he often accompanied me when I golfed. By age 11 he was registered as a junior at the Portage Golf club, the $25.00 seasonal fee included weekly lessons from pro Herb Scarrett. Andrew became a competent golfer, winning club championships and competing in Manitoba junior and a Canadian junior championship.

(This week) Andrew played in the qualifying rounds of the Manitoba Junior golf championship. He shot 80 –76 which put him in14th out of 164 golfers.
(Diary July 20, 1979)

Wendy and Bev played fastball and ringette. I coached girls fastball for about 10 years. Fastball was an intense spring activity, involving two or three nights per week in May and June. Both girls played on local and provincial championship fastball teams.

Tonite our girls pee wee team won the city championship defeating Bruce Buschau's team 14 – 8. He again played only his 9 best players… I used all my players the way I did all season… Bev made a tremendous running catch at centre field in the 6th inning.
(Diary June28, 1979)

In ringette both girls were goalies and played on local and provincial championship teams. Bev played for the Macgregor ringette team for a few years before the game was well developed in Portage. This meant regular trips to Macgregor for practices and games.

Andrew started working at Safeway part time when he was 15; Wendy worked at a florist shop and Bev smelled of popcorn from her work at the local theatre. Academically our children all had the capacity to do well, as is evident in their subsequent education and careers. Bev received the Governor General's award at her grade 12 graduation.

This past weekend spent at Hecla Island Provincial Park. Friday morning Andrew and I golfed the new course there – I shot a 98, Andrew 108. He was not very happy with his score. (Diary, 16 August 1976)

Tena deserves most of the credit for the parenting of our children; her patience, consistency, skill at managing with very few resources and her love and care for the kids was the greatest gift they received.

Church

A billboard in southern Manitoba reads: "You will pay for your sins."
Someone added: "If you have already paid, please ignore this notice."

Despite periodic frustrations with organized religion, we usually attended church. On moving to Portage La Prairie we attended the small Westview Mennonite Brethren (MB) church. When the pastor left after a few years we continued without a pastor. I became chair of the church board and leader in this small congregation.

The provincial MB hierarchy was annoyed that three of four people on the church board were not church members and were of General Conference background. The Manitoba MB conference launched an investigation that involved MB pastors visiting us and pressuring us to join the church. We did not react well to their pressure tactics. People from our church with an MB background pleaded with the conference leadership, arguing that the church simply selected the most competent people for leadership. To no avail; the conference leadership decided that non-members could not serve on elected church positions – they said we might mislead the church. Three of us resigned and the church closed some time later.

In 1978 I wrote:
"When the pastor left… I found myself thrust into a leadership position for which I felt inadequate and unprepared… the church closed because the ecclesiastical hierarchy considered it unacceptable that, among other things, a layman should be functioning in a "ministering" capacity.

This unfortunate and unnecessary ending to a church made us pessimistic about the church as an institution and about church leaders who seemed understanding when we met them individually but who quickly followed the party line when in a group setting: alarming hypocrisy. A redeeming factor was that there were no relational difficulties among those of us in the church. The problems were externally imposed by Mennonite Brethren denominational leaders.

At times I feel very furious and angry that a church organization could be so rigid, so inflexible, and so seemingly in human. I resent many of the things we have been subjected to, many of the accusations that have been thrown at us, or worse still, only hinted at. Unhappiness and dejection were not uncommon feelings this past week… there is the sorrow that comes from seeing the pain and sorrow that people, "Christian" people are capable of causing each other.

How then do, we seek truth? How do we find God's will for ourselves,
individually and collectively? Where do we go from here? Can the damage that has been done be repaired? Where does love and understanding and forgiveness enter in? What would Christ do? Would we all be further ahead if we went to worship elsewhere?

We tend to look at obstacles that come into our pathway as problems,
problems that need to be overcome. Is it possible to see the current situation not as another major problem… but rather as an opportunity for growth…. Do obstacles and problems prevent growth or do they make a different kind of growth possible?

Not all of our names are written in the same church register, for some this a problem. Can we redefine this problem and make it an opportunity…?

Those of us who have been at various meetings with the boards from Winnipeg recently have seen how difficult it is for others to even understand that this church does not function in the usual manner, and of course, their "usual manner" is also right… we have committed the crime of not sticking with tradition.

In conclusion I believe the power of growth is in relationship; relationship to God and relationship to our fellow man. Even when there is disappointment and darkness, even when there is confusion and complexity, the caring and concern of another person results in growth… at least some of this growth I have experienced with you and for this I thank you. (Sermon, May 21, 1972)

We worshipped at home on Sunday mornings for a while but missed the interaction with others. We attended the Evangelical Mennonite church for about two years but found their thinking quite restrictive.

Portage Mennonite Church

In September 1977 Tena and I sent a letter to a number of people inviting them to our house to discuss the possibility of starting a new church. At the first meeting of 10 people, Tony Peters, Menno Enns and I were asked to explore the possibility of renting a building. Six days later, on a rainy Saturday morning we met with Rev. Lloyd Henderson, pastor of the downtown Portage Presbyterian church and of the smaller Crescent Heights chapel in the west end of Portage. We wanted to rent the chapel. Rev. Lloyd Rev. Henderson agreed; we rented the Crescent Heights Chapel for $15.00 per Sunday.

We had our first service on October 16, 1977 with 10 adults and 11 children. We met with the welcoming aroma of coffee brewing at the back of the chapel. It's a miracle that all this happened in a month since our first meeting.

At that first service I spoke about why we met:

- because we share a common faith in Jesus Christ.
- because we are friends and care about each other.
- because we want to grow as Christians.
- because we want to provide our children with an opportunity to study, question, and to examine the call to follow Jesus as Lord.
- because we want to proclaim the triumphs of the Lord – in our lives and in the world.
- because we want to make disciples of ourselves and of others.
- because we are seekers, we have not arrived, not one of us.
- because we are free, we want to live life in the fullness, richness and joy he has promised.

In winter we met in homes for short-term weeknight studies with excellent attendance and participation; serious discussion mixed with a lot of laughter.

After a few years the Presbyterians decided to sell their building and we rented the Seventh Day Adventist church building. We thought this an excellent arrangement; they used the building on Saturday, we on Sunday. After a few years they suggested we needed our own building and we bought the former Alliance church building at 89 – 13 St. NW.

One unusual aspect of our church was the one-year membership feature. Each year we had a service to renew our commitment to God and each other. If one did not re-covenant for another year, church membership lapsed.

Chapter 7. Thailand
1985 – 1988

No one can even begin to think of knowing this country until he has been in it for twenty years. (E. M. Forster, *A Passage to India.*)

Ideal deportment involves acting in a gentle manner, maintaining a 'cool heart', avoiding the expression of anger, hatred, annoyance. On a more practical level, the mechanisms for indirect expression of dismay, annoyance, hatred, are in daily use…. (Conflict or Communication, William Klausner, 1978)

You know it's the hot season when you take shower to cool off, and you resume sweating from the effort of toweling off. (Wanda Sloan)

MCC approved our application and we agreed to work in a refugee camp in Thailand. In preparation for our work we, along with Stu Clarke from MCC, flew to Toronto and Ottawa for refugee related meetings in June 1985. On 15 July 1985, Bev, Tena and I left for Akron Pennsylvania for MCC orientation.

This represents the start of a new phase of our life with all kinds of unexpected new things on the horizon, in many ways a gigantic leap of faith. (Diary, 15 July 1985)

The 23-hour flight from New York took us to Anchorage, Taipai, Hong Kong and finally Bangkok left us with severe jet lag. We left New York on July 28, crossed the international date line, and arrived in Asia on July 3. This meant Tena never had her 50th birthday on July 29. Jake Buhler and Fred Redekop met us at the Bankok airport.

During two weeks of Thai language classes we visited the Royal palace and were part of a small crowd anointed with lustral water by the Thai king while we knelt in an inch of water on the portico. Thais told us such sprinkling was "auspicious" and meant good fortune.

Today was the last day of our language classes… we spent about two hours on telling time – not particularly helpful & also confusing because they divide the day into four 6-hour sections and have different terms for each six hour block.
(Diary, 16 August 1985)

For two weeks in Phanat Nikhom we lived in the large Youth With a Mission (YWAM) home. Ceiling fans, squatter toilets, ants, intense heat, high humidity and a water shortage were part of those early weeks. On September 3 Fred and Shirley Redekop left and we moved into their place in Muuhabaan Phanat, a small two storey place with lots of cockroaches which Tena tried to eliminate one at a time, at night, with a dustpan.

Bev is getting to see a lot of things that she has never seen before – things like rats, cockroaches, centipedes and multipedes and little lizards. The small lizards or jingjots as they are called here live in our house and eat mosquitoes and other bugs. We don't mind them as much as the cockroaches. The cockroaches don't like daylight so we usually make sure we turn the lights on before we walk into a room in the evening. I have found that the dust pan works quite well to kill them.
(Tena, letter to her parents)

The refugee camp, about a half hour drive from Phanat, was set on 140 acres in a rural area. We traveled to and from camp in the American Refugee Committee (ARC) van. The refugee camp consisted of 8,000 – 20,000 people Vietnamese, Khmer, and Laotian refugees.

Teaching refuges destined for Canada about climate, jobs, housing, laws, etc., of Canada was part of our work. We used refugee interpreters; sometimes we wondered about the accuracy of their translations. The Asian education custom is for students not to ask questions; asking the teacher something might embarrass the teacher, if, by chance, he would not know the answer to the question. This would cause the teacher to "lose face" in front of the entire class: a socially unacceptable behaviour.

This day a new era began in our family, Bev left for Canada. After 11 months with MCC and us she was ready to return and pursue her life. In many ways it was an excellent experience for her... at the same time there were few people here her own age... the place seemed empty today and it will take a while to get used to her not being here. For Tena and me the end of active parenting also means the onset of middle age.
(Diary, June 11,1986)

Part of our work was seeking Canadian church sponsorships for refugees no one wanted. Most western countries are selfish when accepting refugees; they want small families, preferably with workable knowledge of English, and the more education the better. The result was that the uneducated, those with few marketable skills, and large families were not wanted by most western countries. These families often asked us to find a sponsor for them. We'd prepare a profile of a family or individual and send it to the MCC office in Winnipeg, from where it would be distributed to provincial MCC offices and to churches. Usually some church would agree to sponsor a refugee family and many families were helped to get to Canada.

In 1988 a group of Canadian members of parliament and senators toured the camp and we got a ride back to Phanat with them. As we were leaving the bus MP Menno Friesen said he

wanted to thank us for showing them around camp and since
Canada is a bilingual country, he would do it in the other language – and proceeded to make his speech in Low German.

Three Dogs and their Nun, Ed Bittenbender and his Birds (1985)

*Tuesday evening mass is held in a small room that opens to the side
of the spacious sanctuary. A dozen people gather for the service,
Roman Catholics who know what to do and say at the right times,
a Jew, and a few Mennonites.*

*Across from us in the unlit sanctuary and three rows from the
back, sits a nun in meditation. She is always there on Tuesday
nights and the dog is there too. He wanders in after her, sitting
behind the last pew till she takes her place, then he stretches out
on the cool stone floor and sleeps. When the nun kneels to pray he
opens his eyes and watches her. His head does not move.*

*Later when she rises to leave his head follows her every move.
Then he slowly follows her out. Last night there were three
dogs, all behaving in the same quiet undisruptive, undoglike
manner. Have they been trained since puppyhood about proper
church behaviour?*

Dogs in the church
*The Sunday morning service at the International Church in
Bangkok begins at 8:00, before the hot Asian sun becomes oppres-
sive. The large sanctuary has doors along one side that open to the
churchyard. Birds continuously fly into the church. Many don't fly
out. They stay for the service. They sit on the ledges on either side
of the church. A few fly to the large cross the front of the church
and sit on it, and sing. Whether it's during Ed Bittenbender's
sermon, during prayer or during music, the birds insist on making
their contribution. They live in the church.*

Birds on the cross, Dogs sleeping in the sanctuary. It baffles my western mind. It's not quite right, animals in the church. Surely there is a time and a place… .

Yet no one seems to mind the birds and the dogs. The birds draw our attention to the cross. The dogs remind us that there is a time to be quiet, even for dogs.

Three dogs and their nun, Ed Bittenbender and his birds. She seems to ignore the dogs, he is not perturbed by the birds. Two servants appear to be at peace with God's creatures. The creatures are there to add to the service or to have their own. (Printed in MCC *Intercom*, June 1986.)

Phyrin Duong 1969 - 1987

It's been a difficult month. On April 30 we arrived at camp, to find Phyrin Duong had hanged himself from a tree in our quad. Burial was the same day in Gapho. This has been a major tragedy. The image of his body swinging in the breeze will remain with me permanently. (Diary, May 24, 1987)

The following article was printed in *The Mennonite*
On Tuesday he told me that our Mennonite Central Committee bicycle had a flat. He wanted to fix it. I was going to bring a new tube from town the next day, but he wanted to fix the old one.

On Wednesday he came with his big smile, he had bought a tube and fixed the bike. I wanted to pay him for the tube but he refused and he jokingly put the money in his shirt pocket He tried to give it back but I wouldn't take it so he went in and put it on the desk where Tena was working, again refusing to keep it. Tena put it inside his Khmer Bible.

Thursday morning we arrived at camp and were told of his death. He hanged himself. Near our buildings. His Bible was where he always put his books when he came to work. The money was still in his bible. Now we know why he didn't need it.

For the past eight months he worked for us as our English-Khmer translator. Competent, dependable, usually cheerful, steady. A pleasure to work with. His story is a tragedy of Khmer proportions. Difficulties began with his family's dislocation by the Khmer Rouge. Phyrin was placed away from his family in a children's camp. When together again the family managed to escape Thailand and the Khao-I-Dang refugee camp was their haven and their hope.

Disappointments continued. Their relatives in the USA had not listed Phyrin's family as their relatives, thus the relationship could not be proven; they were rejected by the USA. Finally they were accepted by Canada and in May 1985 were moved to Phanat Nikhom camp, the last stop before resettlement. They attended the MCC Canadian orientation classes.

They all passed their medicals except Phyrin. He had TB. After over a year of treatment, the family was scheduled ot to leave for Canada on September 27, 1986. The pre-departure medicals indicated a positive sputum for Phyrin. Departure was cancelled by Health and Welfare Canada.

Anger, frustration, exasperation, questions. After a year of treatment with all tests negative, one positive sputum and their hopes were dashed. Lab error was a possibility as was Phyrin's not responding to treatment.

Stronger medication was begun and we were told that the side effects could include depression and emotional outbursts. He soon became quieter and more withdrawn.

Despite considerable efforts by Canadian embassy staff in Bangkok, the medical condition continued to be a problem. Now Ottawa had to decide. We wrote MCC asking them to involve TB specialist Dr. E Hirschfield in this case. And during all of this his tests continued to be negative.

Phyrin often talked with us and medical personnel in camp about this.

Others had TB, were treated, and were now in Canada, yet his family could not go. Why? Some could leave after three months of treatment, yet he was to receive it for six months. Why? When can I go to Canada was his frequent question.

Some weeks ago we were discussing this and I asked Phyrin if he believed that many people here and in Canada were working to get him to go to Canada. With his usual skepticism he said yes, he believed, but he would really believe it when he was able to put his feet on Canadian soil.

When the family was held back from departure last September Phyrin talked about sneaking out of camp and retuning to the Kampuchean border to join the Khmer resistance forces and fight the Vietnamese in Kampuchea. He stayed at camp but often said he wanted to die. It was difficult to give him hope. He sacrificed himself so that the family is free to go to Canada. He is no longer a burden to them. But they will carry this burden the rest of their lives.

He was wrapped in a shroud and placed in a coffin. In our classroom lay his guitar, which he had been playing yesterday, neatly wrapped in a shroud similar to the one that held him.

In the scorching noonday Asian sun at the edge of a Chinese Thai cemetery, near the village of Gapho, his parents, three brothers, one sister along with half a dozen of us gathered for the burial of Phyrin Duong. The coffin was opened and the father uncovered Phyrin's face, knelt beside the coffin clutching a few flowers and prayed for his son. And wept.

While the coffin was lowered into the concrete vault, the parents had consented to a prayer being said and I prayed for God's mercy for this, His departed child.

The coffin was lowered and while we each placed a lighted incense stick in the ground, the concrete was mixed to seal the slab that covered Phyrin's grave.

It was noon, only four hours after we arrived at camp.

It seemed more like a year. Or a lifetime.

The afternoon at our building was quiet. Allison Havill, who introduced Phyrin to the guitar and the Khmer scriptures, brought the saw.

I cut the large branch from a tree near our building. The scar will remain.
Henry Neufeld, Phanat Nikhom, April 30, 1987

May 6, 1987.
To: MOI, UNHCR and Volags
From: Henry Neufeld, MCC
RE: Memorial Services for Phyrin Duong

In memory of Phyrin Duong, who died April 30, 1987, Buddhist ceremonies will be held on Thursday, May 7, commencing at 7:00 a.m. at MCC buildings (L145, Transit).

The family has also requested a Christian service and this is planned for 1:00 p.m., also on Thursday, May 7, at the MCC buildings. Opportunity will be given for individuals to talk about Phyrin and/or the family at this service.

Volags are welcome to participate in this service. ("Volag" means voluntary agency, like MCC)

Phyrin's family left for Canada some months later and settled in Vancouver. Sadly, the "Phyrin solution" was attempted by others in the camp facing similar delays. Phyrin's death was reported in both Bangkok English language daily papers, *The Bangkok Post* and *The Nation*.

In an ironic and sadistic act, the Canadian embassy in Bangkok received clearance for Phyrin to emigrate seven days after his death. Officials in Ottawa knew of Phyrin's death, why they would grant him medical clearance, knowing he had died, boggles the mind.

Dr. Earl Herschfield a TB specialist in Winnipeg and one of the architects of Canadian medical policy for immigrants with TB, placed responsibility for the delay in Phyrin's departure with a specific doctor working for Health and Welfare Canada. Dr. Hershfield visited our camp in November 1986, spoke with Phyrin, reviewed his medical records and told us that if Phyrin's family was sent toWinnipeg, he would be willing to follow up and treat Phyrin.

Letter from Ray Nott, Powell, Wyoming, June 8, 1987. (Ray and Nancianna Nott were managers of the Christian Guest House, Bangkok.)

It was good to hear from you. It was like a short visit… which we miss so much. But we were really shook and saddened by the tragic death of Phyrin Duong. We read the account over and over, and shook our heads. Our eyes filled with tears, and felt like something good had gone from the world. Another example of poor timing. Another example of 'too late with too little.' And Phyrin was caught. And grief stretches into a tragedy.

Then we thought about you two… going there to do what needs to be done… to do your best. I suppose that's one reason we all go to Thailand. I think there's a time when you zero in on your life and we get comfortable. We get familiar with our abilities and we can pretty well tell how things are going to unfold. Then one day we look around and we know who's going to show up for the game. It's all so predictable. And you begin to wonder "Is there more around the corner?" or is there something completely different?" So you break away. You go off on a different tack. You go to Thailand.

But you didn't expect this to happen. Nobody does. What's impor-tant is that you were there. As Mordecai said to Esther, "For such a time as this, you have come." When I read your account, I was glad that you were there. And that we had the opportunity to know you both.

Nobody will really understand why you went and what you've been through. Nobody, except you two and Beverly and a handful of others you've grown close to in Thailand. Other than that, no one can comprehend.

#51 (Printed in MCC Intercom May 1988)

She noticed me approaching and came running. As I got off the bicycle she desperately clutched my arm. Her tears, repeatedly wiped with a sarong, told the story. She led me to the bamboo hut near the hospital, where her husband's body lay on a stretcher propped up by boxes on a gravel floor. She uncovered his face for me.

He had died in his sleep early that morning; he had been ill for some time. She lit another candle and placed it near the stretcher along with the joss sticks. We stood there in silence, her fingers digging into my arm.

A few hours later she, her three children, two escorts from the camp and I were in a pick-up on our way to the cemetery. We approached a series of simple concrete vaults for the poor and the refugees in the far corner, well away from the elaborate Chinese graves. Our escorts took us to the vault with the lid partly open so we could see the coffin. Mother and children lit candles and joss sticks while saying prayers. The funeral service had begun.

Initially the man had had tuberculosis that went untreated. Then his high blood pressure made air travel unsafe and later therapy for lung cancer seemed to weaken his body and spirit. When his daughter spent time with him in the Bangkok hospital, he was mildly annoyed. Her presence meant he was ill; returning to camp would signify improved health and imminent departure for Canada.

A few weeks ago as we were leaving camp we noticed him sitting beside the road, alone. He had just returned from Bangkok and lacked energy to walk home after a long tiring ride. He had been dropped off at the administration building with no apparent thought of giving him a ride home. We helped him to a table and arranged for one of his daughters to come help him home.

The five-minute funeral service was over, our escorts were ready to leave. The teenage daughter rose from her prayer, her eyes scanning the area, one of those 'if I ever come here again how will I recognize this place' looks. Her eyes came back to the row of vaults and stopped at her father's. They were numbered. Silently she mouthed it: 51.

Southeast Asia Refugees, Bulletin # 15 May 1988

During our time in Thailand I wrote periodic letters to Canadian MCC offices about the refugee situation; below is an excerpt from the last letter. MCC asked us to stop in Ottawa on our return to Canada to debrief Canadian government officials about our experience; then MCC cancelled our Ottawa visit, apparently because observations in this bulletin did not coincide with MCC's thinking. We were never told what parts of the report were unacceptable to MCC. Meanwhile, this bulletin had been sent to Ottawa by Canadian Immigration staff in Bangkok. In fall 1988 Ottawa officials told me that this bulletin was making the rounds in the federal bureaucracy and was generating some excellent discussion.

SOUTHEAST ASIA REFUGEES. BULLETIN #15. MAY 1988
Observations

After almost three years here we have some comments to make about the asylum seekers and related matters.

The reasons people flee their own countries are primarily caused by man rather than by nature: i.e., persecution, exploitation, war, etc. The profound imbalance in world economies combined with suppression and exploitation result in people wanting to leave their homeland.

Asylum seekers are used as political, economic and military pawns. Note the tremendous variation in how Khmer, Lao and Vietnamese asylum seekers are treated, both by Thailand and by resettlement countries.

Some people and some countries profit financially from refugees.

Refugee camps, over a period of time, create economic, emotional, and social problems. They foster dependence and lethargy. Camps train people in helplessness.

Resettlement of refugees, when it involves extreme cultural upheaval should only be an emergency solution, not a long range plan. There is something immoral about shifting large groups of people to a foreign culture; it represents too much upheaval. Refugees represent the failure to find political solutions to Indochinese conflicts dating back hundreds of years.

In discussing asylum seekers in Thailand, one must consider separately the Laotians, Khmer, Vietnamese and Karen, taking onto account the unique economic, political and military factors of each country. These considerations should reflect the policy of resettlement countries.

It is difficult to understand Canada's foreign policy toward Vietnam, in essence it seems to be that Canadian aid is not available to Vietnam until Vietnamese forces withdraw from Kampuchea. If the Vietnamese withdraw the Khmer Rouge would likely return to power and it seems hard to understand that Canada would support the return of the KR. Maybe it's time to acknowledge that the Vietnamese did the world a favour by driving out the Khmer Rouge. Now we should be attempting to ensure a peaceful Kampuchea, not a return of the Khmer Rouge. A Canadian position that does not necessarily follow that of the USA would be desirable.

Canada seems to have a schizophrenic policy toward Vietnamese who want to leave their homeland: to leave directly from Ho Chi Minh City for Canada means they must first meet stringent immigration criteria, however if they get to Thailand they can be readily accepted for resettlement as refugees with no immigration criteria to meet. And we wonder why Vietnamese keep coming to Thailand.

Canada should apply the UNHCR definition of a refugee to all who apply to go to Canada, with the possible exception of family reunification cases.

Since many asylum seekers in Thailand are using the refugee system as an immigration system, there will likely be a major backlash toward all asylum seekers and the suffering of genuine refuges will increase. There seems to be an abuse of the refugee system on a major scale.

The 1979 Geneva conference on Indochinese refugees was based on three premises:
1. anyone from Kampuchea, Laos or Vietnam is a refugee,
2. SE Asian asylum countries will not be left with a residual refugee population.
3. Resettlement will solve the refugee problem
It is time for another conference, new assumptions, and new strategies.

Canadian churches who sponsor refugees should define criteria according to which they will apply to sponsor refugees, taking into consideration the GLOBAL refugee situation. The need for sponsorships from other parts of the world might be far greater than from SE Asia.

MCC is in a unique position to use established work in Laos, Kampuchea, and Vietnam to begin to speak to governments (Canada and USA) about refugee causing situations and measures which could be taken to decrease the flow of asylum seekers, and to facilitate repatriation.

It is anticipated that in 1988 more asylum seekers will arrive in Canada than in all of SE Asia.

Seeking asylum throughout the world will likely increase in the next decade. As Christians it is important to remember that God has been our refuge throughout all generations; man's quest will continue until we find our rest in God.

Leaving Thailand

Jake Buhler was our MCC country director during our first two years in Thailand. When we left he handed us a letter with instructions not to open it until we were airborne. Excerpts appear below.

Dear Tena and Henry:
So end three years of refugee work with MCC. Time to reflect on what it has meant to you. Time to reflect on what you may have meant to others. On the former – only you can say; on the latter - only we and others can answer.

There was the beginning. Two experienced people and one daughter who arrived…. Thailand was new. Asia was new. But living was not new.

So you learned a lot of things quickly…. You learned that to be logical is to accept that which is not logical.

There were disappointments when systems stood in the way of assisting refugees. And at times there was tragedy when blocked systems and careless people caused people to take their own lives.

You were there. You saw the agony. You helped those who were in agony… .

You adjusted and maintained a middle way: you got on with the evangelicals and maintained respect; you commanded the respect of the refugees who felt your assistance time after time; you were consistent and methodical and thought of well by the immigration folks at the Canadian Embassy; you were sensible about culture and got on well with those in the market, at the photo shop, at the bus station.

You spoke not so much but lived quite a lot. One Thai said at your farewell "you lived like a Jesus way." The finest tribute of all.

So as you leave, do note that we as former MCC colleagues enjoyed your humour, agonized when you agonized, rejoiced when you rejoiced. We noted your stability, your commitment and your ability to empathize without losing sight of reality.

We will miss you, of course. But the world isn't so big. We will probably meet again and talk of old things… and new things.

Mass
We often attended the Tuesday night small gathering of foreigners at the Roman Catholic church where one of the priests who worked at the refugee camp said mass. Were invited to participate fully. "We're here to serve all Christians, said Father Tom. Shortly before leaving Thailand the priest said a special mass for us: a moving and humbling experience.

Letters from Thailand (written to friends and family)
January 25, 1986.
The other night when we got home from the camp there was a note stuck on our gate that if we didn't pay our electricity bill by noon they'd cut our power. This I learned after I found someone who could read Thai and speak English (a difficult combination), but no one seemed to know exactly where to pay the bill, finally someone said we should go up a lane near the hotel where there was a gate where the electric city (as they call electricity) was

*located. We've been here 6 months and I've never seen the hotel!
The next day Tena and Bev got a Thai girl to show them where to
go and paid the bill…. Usually the guy comes to our gate at either
6:00 a.m. or 7:00 p.m. and yells, so we go out to pay for water or
electricity and the guy stops yelling and goes away.* (Henry)

May 2, 1986
*I talked with one 12 year old (Vietnamese) boy… who is the only
survivor from a boat of 23 people, the others were all killed or
thrown overboard. He was thrown over as well, but swam after
the boat and climbed back on, they let him rest, then threw him
over, he swam after the boat and climbed on again, same thing,
then they finally let him stay on board.* (Henry)

May 24, 1986
*The week of May 12 –17 we were on a tour of refugee camps in
northern Thailand… the hilltribe refugees are quite a different
bunch… Opium smoking is not uncommon, bras seem to be
unknown, (or inconvenient, as Tena says) and medicine men are
used frequently. I heard a medicine man shouting and carrying
on, I peered through the bamboo to get a look and got invited in
to stay and watch. He was dancing on a bench, singing, shouting,
whistling, jumping and slapping his bare feet on the bench for
about an hour while I was there. I left and checked about half an
hour later and he was still going strong. He had a hood over his
face so he couldn't see who was there. The six or so people who
sat around were either dozing, smoking a long bamboo pipe, or
jus appeared bored with the whole exercise, the purpose of which I
never discovered.*

June 20, 1986
*The Lao couple with the cute little girl are going on June 22 to
Ottawa. When I told them they were delighted, she gave me two
hearty hugs (which seems surprising for Asians) and dad gave me
23 wais, then knelt down and put his arms around my knees and
hugged them. Another first for me and I didn't know what to do,
but finally he got up. They are very grateful….*

Kunthea translated for Laurie (ARC nurse) who came to do a family planning lecture for Mom's afternoon Khmer ladies, and Laurie was impressed with how well she translated. Despite that none of them looked very interested and all rushed off to repopulate Battambang or Siem Riep as quickly as possible.

August 3, 1986
I am amazed some days that I can cope with this work 5 days a week but then I don't have as many responsibilities outside of work hours. We are managing to work together quite well and enjoy it, something I often wondered about. (Tena)

August 10, 1986 (letter to Bev)
Yesterday as we were finishing supper Deng (our laundry lady), her sister and her husband and three kids arrived with some khanom – sticky rice with some slimy stuff on top and a little bag of coconut milk – Mom and I ate the whole thing right after they left. I took a picture of the six of them on the motorbike.

August 29, 1986
I had dengue fever which started Aug, 18; it's given to one by the mosquito. It starts with extreme headaches, high fever, and every joint, muscle and whatever else hurting. After few days of this you breakout in a rash which becomes very itchy. You need to take anti-histamines but I did not have any so spent a few sleepless nights before we got some. There is a loss of appetite, diarrhea, and depression that accompanies all this so there si much wishing to be anywhere but where you happen to find yourself. It is amazing how you miss things like ginger ale, apple juice, canned soups, a comfortable chair and being able top go to a Dr. who speaks English. You become immune to the strain that you have and there are 3 more varieties. Henry has not had it and was a little concerned that he might get it…. I'm alright now except my skin is still very sensitive and I still have aches in my legs and feet. The other thing… is that you have a lot of pain behind the eyes. So reading was very difficult – the bright sun here doesn't help…. (Tena)

September 13, 1986

The BBC (radio) *news carried the items about the Sri Lankans going to Newfoundland some time ago…. From where we sit the decision to let them stay in Canada was not a wise move. There are thousands of people out here who would do anything they could to get to Canada or some other western country, and this move to let them stay is a clear message to others that this is a fast way to beat a long immigration system. They should be sent back to Germany and made to apply to come to Canada the way any other immigrant has to….* (Henry)

December 27, 1986.
Tomorrow night we're going to a marriage celebration for one of the American girls who works here who recently married a Thai fellow. His father died rather suddenly in summer, and so they had to either get married within 3 months of his death or wait for three years to get married. In the first three months after his death his spirit is still around, then it is en route to its next life (reincarnation) and it is not good to get married while the spirit is en route. The widow went to a monk to ask him to ask the spirit of the deceased husband if it was ok for the son to marry the girl. Then spirit asked if it was "that foreign girl" and when told it was, the spirit gave its approval for the marriage. So they were married in Buddhist ceremony in summer and here and now her parents are coming and they'll have a wedding celebration tomorrow evening. Should be interesting. (Henry)

January 24, 1987 (Tena's letter to Bev about Henry & Andrew's golf at Hua Hin.)
Dad and Andrew golfed on Monday; they each had a caddy. Dad was assigned an old granny and Andrew had a young shy girl. The old granny laughed at Dad's shots, ordered Coke and had him pay, and asked for a tip because she wanted to buy lunch.

July 21, 1987.
On our anniversary we went for a motorcycle ride in the moonlight, it was quite romantic, really, with Tena's arms wrapped around my waist, and me trying to keep my mouth shut so it didn't fill with bugs and we almost ran over a rat which was traveling across the road from one rice field to another.

October 1987
We visited refugees who are in the Bangkok General Hospital for medical treatment. They seemed very lonely and sad, missing families a lot. For many there is a language barrier and despite kind nursing staff they have little understanding of what's happening to them or why. We brought food and messages from families at camp and this seemed to be much appreciated.

October 1987
The US senate approved a bill to resettle 28.000 more Indochinese refugees. Thailand gets $5 million for "affected Thai villages," $2 million for training security forces on the Thai/Kampuchea border, and $5 million for educational program for refugees. The Thais must be enjoying this immensely.

November 4, 1987
On Thanksgiving Sunday we had a group of (Canadian) parliamentarians visit us at camp. They were in Thailand for some meetings and had requested to see a refugee camp. They gave us a ride to Phanat in their chartered bus and as we were ready to get off Benno Friesen (MP from Surrey B.C.) took the mike and said that he wanted to say a few things to us and since Canada was a bilingual country, he would do it in the other language. He proceeded to speak in Low German; a few Francophones looked a little startled.

November 4, 1987
While in Bangkok we also visited some refugees in hospital… many refugees here have thyroid problems and one woman had had surgery. The nurse told us she had a "noodle" removed. It took a few minutes until we realized she meant nodule.

November 30, 1987 (from a letter to Julie Sawatsky, aged 9)
We got home from work just after 5:00, then I went to the post office on the motorcycle and also did a few other errands. Sometimes when I come home from the post office I stop and buy a bag of fried bananas, there's a guy has a wok and fries them out on and I just pull up and show him four fingers and he knows that

means four baht (about 20 cents) and he puts enough bananas in bag for me and I come home and Tena says why did you buy those cause I'm going to get fat, but she eats one or two or three anyway.

Usually it's too hot to bake, but if Tena makes bread or something and leaves it on the table, a jingjot (lizard, about four inches long) will go and nibble a bit of bread and Tena chases him away. We have about six of them that share the house with us. They're ok because they're afraid of people. When we first came here I didn't like them, now I think they're ok, and maybe we'll bring one home as a pet.

Tonight the water guy came down our street, he comes every Monday and Thursday night to sell clean drinking water. He comes on those two nights unless it rains, then he doesn't come at all, but nobody knows why. Maybe he just doesn't want to get wet.

November 22, 1987
Tena and Diane (American physical rehab worker) are trying to make some guava jelly, but since neither has a recipe and they each have a poor memory, the result could be rather intriguing, and I'll likely have to eat it. Right now it smells ok, but it looks like elephant's milk.

December 29, 1987 (letter to Bev)
On Christmas day we went to Bangkok and were sort of tired so we decided to have a quiet dinner and relax – it didn't quite work out that way... as we walked back into the Christian Guest House a couple from Canada who are visiting were inside the office; he was on the phone to his Dad in the US and she whispered to us to stick around. To put it briefly, he was in a full blown paranoid psychosis, telling his Dad he was married to a spy, saying people had drugged him etc., etc. I went with him to the hospital in the ambulance, then when the doc wanted him to go upstairs and see the psychiatrist, he turned to me and said, "Why are you doing this to me?" and ran off at full tilt down Silom towards Patpong, an orderly and me after him. I got tired and gave up, the orderly was smart, he got a tuktuk to follow him and hollerd at some motorcycle cops as he went by.

So the cops took him to the police station at Suan Phlu, phoned the Guest House; a Thai staff and I went to get him. I wanted the cops to escort the guy to the hospital since I knew he'd take off on us. The cops took one look at him, and figured he looked alright so they were going to get a hearse (the only vehicle available) to take us. I refused, thinking that putting a paranoid in a hearse was not a great idea. Finally an ambulance arrived but of course our friend refused to get in. They brought him a glass of water and he told me to drink it (he refused to touch it) because it had truth serum in it, so I drank it and have been honest ever since. "I have my rights, I'm an American, I want to se the ambassador," he said. At one point he asked me "Who do you work for?" I said "MCC, you remember the barbecue you were at with other MCC'ers a few weeks ago." "But who do you really work for?" he asked. "I work for God," I said. His face brightened noticeably.

The cops said come in the pickup truck, with "Police" written on the side. He agreed. He said he trusted the cops because he had been watching them operate. At the Bangkok Nursing Home (hospital) the cops dropped us off and left as quickly as they could. We walk into the Nursing home, an orderly appears. The Thai orderly is about 5'1", my friend is over 6' tall. "I have my rights," he says to the orderly. The orderly's English is passable, but he asks him to repeat what he said. "I have my rights." The orderly responds: "Sure, tonight you sleep here and tomorrow we get you paper and then you can write." I thought I was in a Monty Python skit.

He went upstairs, asked for water, the nurses gave him a pill, and he slept. We waited for the doc, and were back at the Guest House by 2:00 a.m. The couple left Thailand a few days later.

February 13, 1988.
The Thais and Lao are fighting about three hills which they both want… they're starting to use some heavy artillery. Now Laos has asked to negotiate and the Thai chief of national security responded: "It is better that Thailand and Laos can talk. Talking while shooting is far better than shooting without talking."

February 13, 1988

The Bangkok Post *reported on an upcoming beauty pageant: "…*
only shapely girls with beautiful legs will win… the contestants
will be wearing sunglasses or a mask to allow the judges to concen-
trate only on their figure and legs."

April 12, 1988
Sunday morning I went to RC mass and Tena stayed home and
meditated over some mango jam, which turned out absolutely deli-
cious, so she feels quite appropriately self righteous about skipping
mass, and I'm planning to write the Pope about her and send him
some jam as well. She tried to give our laundry woman some jam
and she smiled and said Thais don't eat "yam" which is as close
to English as she'll ever get. Back to the mass, Father Olivier was
talking about the disciple Thomas not believing that Jesus had
risen from the tomb and referred to Thomas as a "headblock"
which caused a few of us to wonder, then he got it right and called
him a blockhead. (Henry)

June 15, 1988
We took Jean (MacDonald) to "Cabbages and Condoms," an
excellent Thai restaurant operated by Meechai, the family plan-
ning man. The food was great and if one so desired there were
drinks available at the "Vasectomy bar." Jean Bought some
interesting T shirts there and you might ask her to model them for
you. (Henry)

Herman and Sara Neufeld 25th anniversary, 1946.
Back:Hilda and Margaret
Front: Henry and John"

Henry age 20

Tena Suderman, age 21

Sara and Herman Neufeld (1971)

Henry and Tena Suderman wedding, 1960
Left:Frank and Mary Suderman, Henry and
Tena, Sara and Herman Neufeld

Standing: Jake Bergen, Tena and Henry Neufeld, John and
Anne Neufeld, John Warkentin. Seated: Margaret Bergen,
Sara and Herman Neufeld, Hilda Warkentin. (1971)

Wendy, Andrew, Tena, Henry holding Beverly (1968)

Henry, Tena, Andrew, Beverly, Wendy (1970)

Beverly, Wendy, Tena, Henry , Andrew (August 1970)

The four Neufelds, John, Henry, Hilda and Margaret (2005)

Henry's childhood home, 24277 58 Ave, Aldergrove, BC.

Andrew at our Saskatoon home, 118 13 St E (1966)

Our Portage la Prairie home, 54 5St SE.

Our home in Phanat Nikhom, Thailand, 1988.

Our Ladner home, 4456 62 Street, Delta., BC.

Buddhist temple, Phanat Nikhom, Thailand.

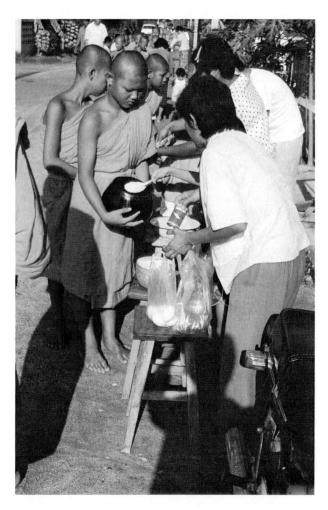

Buddhist novices receiving food, Phanat Nikhom, 1988

Tena, rice planting time, Thailand (1987)

Alain Theault (Canadian embassy), Benno Friesen (Canadian MP), Tena. Phanat Nikhom refugee camp. (1987)

Henry, Michelle Hocke, Jean-Pierre Hocke, UN High Commissioner for Refugees,. Phanat Nikhom refugee camp. (1987)

Refugee camp technology, Hmong camp, northern Thailand.

Food distribution day, Site #2 on the
Thai – Cambodian border.

Shall we cross the Mekong?

Gordon Fairweather, Chair of the Immigration and Refugee
Board at Henry's swearing in ceremony,Vancouver. (1988.)

Tena and Henry. (2007)

Chapter 8. Manitoba, The Third Time: 1988

When we returned a few weeks ago and started unpacking our boxes, we were somewhat overwhelmed with the amount of things we had packed away; we thought we had cleaned up rather well. But after three years of living with minimal but adequate provisions, we found there was a lot we didn't need. Maybe that is one of our dilemmas – we have confused NEEDS and WANTS to the point where we now need things which years ago we only dreamed of having.
(Address to MCC Manitoba alumni, 18 August 1988.)

En route to Canada in late July 1988 we spent a weekend in Geneva meeting with Quakers and MCC Europe regarding refugee related work there. We arrived in Toronto, spent a few days with Wendy & Kevin, and then returned to Portage la Prairie. We stayed with Andy and Kathy for a weekend until Jean MacDonald, who had rented out house, moved out.

On August 2, 1988 I walked (we had no car) to the local telephone office to apply for a phone. I was asked for a driver's license as identification; I said I had none (mine expired while we were in Thailand) but offered my Canadian passport. She said it was not acceptable, I needed a driver's license. I was dumbfounded; my passport enabled me to travel around the world was not sufficient. I realized we were back to small town Canada. I walked to the provincial government office, readily got my driver's license, then back to the telephone office and was approved for a phone.

The first call on our newly activated phone was from Peter Harder in Ottawa. Peter was the Executive Director of the newly formed Immigration and Refugee Board (IRB). Peter offered me a five-year appointment with the new IRB in Vancouver. I was almost speechless and told him I'd need to think about this.

Some say one should not change jobs as one ages, I was in my early 50's and we had three options: Tena and I both had jobs in Portage to return to; we were offered an MCC/Quaker position in Geneva, and now the IRB job in Vancouver. Staying in Portage would have been the safe thing to do – a familiar place, job security and stability - likely until retirement. The Geneva option was attractive because it provided an opportunity to continue in refugee related work and to live in Europe. Geneva would mean more voluntary service, and that had implications for our pensions. Vancouver was desirable since we often talked of moving back to BC, Tena especially wanted to return there. Given the higher cost of housing and relatively low social work salaries, earlier consideration of moving to BC was unrealistic. This new opportunity looked great, yet… what if I was not reappointed after five years? I'd be in my late 50's seeking another job. There are risks in venturing to a new place.

We chose the Vancouver option, realizing this was a once-in-a-lifetime opportunity. We spent the Labour Day (1988) weekend in Vancouver looking for a house, finally finding one at 4456 - 62 Street, Delta (Ladner) for $169,000. While in Vancouver our Portage realtor phoned to say he had an offer on our house that we accepted.

We left Manitoba in late October, stopping in Pincher Creek and Red Deer to visit refugees we had known in Thailand. Our Manitoba years were over.

After returning from Thailand we received many letters from refugees.

Toronto, May 27, 1988.
Dear Mr. And Mrs. Henry.
It has taken me so long to response to your letter. I am terribly sorry. Time has been occupied since I started to work. Work, work, and work to make a living. Some work very hard, some take it very easy. I am in the first group! I have paid all the debt I owed and been able to manage our lives. To me the life here is good. Work and earn money, work more, earn more, every people has choice that sounds fair enough. But I am concerned about others… that they have to study English more.

I've met some folks from P.N. (Phanat Nikhom refugee camp) most of them complain of the language and hard work. Basically their aptitudes to adapt to new society are impaired by their language comprehension.

I'd like to say something about beautiful Canada. I came in late winter, all the trees looked dead. Only the snow which beautified the country. Everything was white and pure. It's cold but never mind. Then one day I don't remember exactly what date I found that I had to unzip my coat when walking. I guessed spring is coming. The grasses are very fast. One week later they covered the green with a pleasantly green color. Then trees keep on budding, flowers blooming.

I've just been laid off due to a shortage of orders. In the meantime I'm hunting for a temporary job, including catching worms. People make lots of money but to me it's awful! I went one night and nearly got sick by pushing myself to stay awake looking for worms. Ahhhhh!!!!! It's a good job for those who don't know English.

I miss P. Nak but, sorry I don't like to live there.
When you get to Toronto, if possible, please drop by our place.

Sincerely,

K Anh.

Dear Sir: (November 1988)
I had the pleasure to see you during your working period in MCC
office in Transit Centre, Phanat Nikhom Camp. In the meanwhile
I got much difficulties with my resettlement and stayed in Camp
for a length of time, nearly three years. My case could not be con-
sidered for resettlement in the USA… so I was very worried and
sad then. However, fortunately obtaining your great favor, you're
very kind in assisting me for resettlement in Canada. You tried all
your best discussing with Mr. Allan (Team Leader of Canadian
delegation) before you left Phanat Nikhom Camp.

Now, I would like to inform you a very good news: I was accepted
by Canadian delegation on the 3th Oct. 1988. I'm really glad and
grateful to you, you helped me get a new life full of prospects in my
future. I don't know how to express my gratitude only that I will
become a good canadian citizen and exert myself to contribute my
society in my future.

In order to acknowledge your kind assistance on me, I just write to
you and thank you from the bottom of my heart and I'll pray for
you everyday and night that God will bless you.

With kind regards,

Nee Toan

On returning to Canada in July 1988 we visited a family in
Toronto who had just arrived from Thailand. When board-
ing a Pakistan International flight to Singapore the family had
been searched by Pakistani staff and a piece of gold taken from
the father, The airlines claimed it looked like a large bullet
and would be returned to the family on arrival in Toronto.
In Toronto no one knew anything about it. The gold was the
family's life savings – valued at about $5,000.

When we arrive at our Manitoba home I wrote the
Intergovernmental Committee for Migration ICM (the
agency which arranges flights for refugees) with a copy to
the Canadian embassy in Bangkok outlining the family's

experience. Mr. Cliff Shaw at the Canadian Embassy was upset about this incident and told ICM that no Canadian bound refugee should be booked to fly on PIA.

I was not optimistic about getting any compensation for the family and felt my efforts were a waste of time. In February 1989 we received a letter from ICM enclosing a letter from PIA:

After having investigated the matter through all possible sources, we have not been able to pin point responsibilities or even ascertain the alleged confiscation of the valuables. This is purely because a number of agencies are involved in handling security at Bangkok airport.

However in view of PIA's long association with ICM in transporting Refugees Traffic, we are prepared to make an ex-gratia payment of Baht 100,000. To Mr. Ung purely as a gesture of good will and on humanitarian grounds.

With this settlement we hope this unfortunate episode will be closed and the transportation of Refugees on BKK/SIN sector of PIA would resume as a reciprocal gesture from ICM/ Canadian Embassy.

Yours sincerely,

Z. Q. Sadique
Manager, Thailand.

I phoned the family in Toronto that evening and asked Sreng if they understood the letter. "Yes, they're going to send us some money and my father says thank you."

Chapter 9. B.C., The Last Time: 1988 –

In October the fogs would roll in; the city below a glowing, foaming prairie of white light, Lions Gate Bridge would puncture through that light, glowing gold, offering transport into that other luminous area. (Douglas Coupland)

BC welcomed us on a rainy day in late October 1988. We stayed with Jake & Margaret Bergen in White Rock for a few days till our furniture arrived, then moved into our new Ladner home at 4456 62 Street.

We attended Peace Mennonite Church in Richmond for a few years but were more attracted to the smaller Point Grey Inter Mennonite Fellowship in Vancouver and began attending there in 1992. This group met in the chapel of the Menno Simons Centre, a former convent turned into a student residence near UBC. This group's choral type singing provided a beautiful avenue of worship. With no pastor the members took on more responsibilities and the response time after the sermon provided feedback and meaningful interaction. I was Moderator of the congregation for four years and also worked on arranging Sunday speakers.

Immigrations and Refugee Board: Convention Refugee Determination Division

Work at the Vancouver office of the Immigration and Refugee Board (IRB) involved quasi-judicial hearings for people who came to Canada and claimed refugee status.. The international (UNHCR) definition of a "Convention refugee" is based on a person having a well-founded fear of persecution in their country of origin to such an extent that they fear returning to their homeland.

Two member panels heard each case, and in the event of a disagreement on the decision to grant refugee status, the decision went in favour of the refugee claimant.

If one panel member believed the person was a refugee, the claimant was granted refugee status.

If we decided the person was a "Convention refugee" we merely needed to sign a statement to that effect. If we decided claimant was not a Convention refugee we had to write detailed reasons for our decision; decisions which, on appeal to the Federal Court, were subject to thorough reexamination. This represented a fundamental flaw in the system; if a member didn't want to spend hours writing a decision, one merely said "yes" to the refugee claimant and no other work was required. Fortunately, we had a conscientious group in Vancouver and this rarely happened.

I faced an ethical dilemma early in this job: Tena and I had just come from Thailand where we saw thousands in refugee camps with no prospect of returning home or resettlement anywhere. Now in Canada I spent hours (sometimes days) deciding one case. This seemed a badly skewed system. Refugee claimants arriving in Canada received government funded services: housing, legal costs, welfare, etc., plus costly hearings (at the time it was estimated that it cost about $50,000 to decide one case at the IRB) while, in comparison, those in UN refugee camps around the world got virtually no help.

The primary difference was that those who managed to arrive in Canada were given access to a Canadian system that provided them with financial aid as well as legal aid services. These refugee claimants were able to get to Canada; they had access to either their own money, or by borrowed money from "agents" who helped them get false documents and airline tickets to get here. The message internationally was clear: get your feet onto Canadian soil and you'll likely be able to stay in Canada. People with no access to assets and no capacity to indenture themselves for years were left in camps. The Canadian refugee system favoured those with money or access to money who could get to Canada.

I resolved the dilemma by acknowledging that, rightly or wrongly, there was one method of dealing with refugees who lived abroad and another for those who arrived in Canada; I happened to work in the IRB system that dealt with refugee claimants arriving in Canada.

A fundamental flaw in the refugee system is that anyone who gets here can say the magic words "I'm a refugee" at the Canadian port of entry and immediately have access to an array of services. Colleagues told me, for instance, if someone in the Punjab wants to come, to Canada, they are often asked by people smugglers if they want to go as a refugee or as an immigrant. The main difference is that the refugee system costs more (paying the agent for false documents, etc.) while the immigration system is slower, often years slower. The refugee system is used, or more accurately abused, as a faster alternative to the lengthy immigration process. Using the refugee route as an immigration system clogs the refugee stream, creating a backlog and delaying the processing of genuine refugees.

How to fix this system? The most effective and radical measure would be to allow no one to enter Canada and make a refugee claim. All refugees coming to Canada would be processed abroad, largely from the pools of millions currently in UNHCR refugee camps. This would ensure that the needy – especially women and children – would be resettled in Canada as refugees rather than those who have access to funds.

Virtually all refugee claimants were represented by lawyers; this usually helped focus the case on key issues, though at times lawyers could become argumentative, verbose, and obstructionist, seeking to delay or prolong hearings. The Vancouver's Immigration lawyers group found that fewer refugees from the same source countries were accepted in Vancouver than in Toronto and Montreal. The lawyers began a lobbying effort, suggesting that Vancouver IRB members were much "tougher" than other IRB members and that was unfair.

I'm sitting here at one of the federal penitentiaries waiting for the prisoner to be brought out for his hearing – he claims to be a refugee – an insight which only came upon him like a flash of lightning after he began serving his life sentence for the not insignificant crime of murder. For whatever reason he does not wish to be deported to homeland, where, quite possibly, murderers are treated less kindly than in Canada.
(Letter to Bev, 22 June 1989)

BIAS AGANSIT REFUGEE CLAIMS CHARGED
(Vancouver Sun headline, 10 September, 1993)
…Rankin and Matas (lawyers) *said four members of the Vancouver CRDD… have especially low rates of acceptance of refugees…. Rankin said the "worst records," meaning the lowest acceptance rates were recorded by Charles Groos with 12 percent acceptance after 106 determinations, Charles Paris with 16 per cent after 96, Lynda-May Angus with 19 per cent after 86, and Henry Neufeld with19 per cent after 113.*
None of the four members could be reached for comment.

Immigration lawyers lobbied against reappointment of 'rigorous' board members. (Vancouver Sun headline, 14 October, 1994)
The lawyers, who make their living representing immigrants and refugee claimants, wrote to board chair Nurjehan Mawani and Marchi urging them not to re-appoint these members, who

reportedly conducted the most rigorous hearings.... Seven of the nine members have been dumped....

Neufeld, another of the seven members who failed to get re-appointment, declined Thursday to speculate about the reason.

But he said he has worked extensively in refugee camps in Thailand for the Mennonite Central Committee, and felt there was a great difference between those refugees unable reach Canada and the claimants who "have the money and means to get here."

The lawyers developed a crude rating scale of IRB members and said that six of us (including me) should be replaced because of our high number of negative decisions. This made headlines in the *Vancouver Sun*. The immigration lawyers were eventually given a slap on the wrist by the law society for their actions. One lawyer sent me a handwritten apology.

I am writing to personally apologize for any hurt, anger, pain, confusion or disappointment the events of recent days may have caused you. I ask that you please forgive me. Although I am some-times passionately rash, I would never knowingly cause what these events have triggered, I count you as a friend and respect you as a colleague....
With sincerest apologies,
Kim Stagg. (14 February 1994)

Tensions between the Vancouver office and head office increased. I was in Ottawa in February 1994 and during lunch with an Assistant Deputy Minister I mentioned that there was no support from head office for Vancouver members being publicly attacked by lawyers. He said: "How can we support you with your (low) acceptance rates?" At that point I realized our fate was sealed and some of us would not be reappointed.

To the criticism that we made too many negative decisions we simply stated that virtually all of these decisions were appealed to the Federal Court. In six years, hearing about 100 cases a year, I had about five cases sent back by the Federal

Court for rehearing. None of my decisions were overturned by the higher courts. Lawyers told me this was an impressive record.

One lawyer told a colleague that he was embarrassed about all the tales his refugee claimants told us in the hearings. Another lawyer, quite critical of our low acceptance rates, was later appointed to the IRB. His acceptance rate quickly declined and he was called 'Dr. No.'

Late in the evening of August 31,1994, a few hours before my term ended, I spoke with my superior, Emer Robles, who advised me that I was not reappointed. A similar fate awaited a number of my colleagues.

Thus ended six years of the best work experience I've had. While challenging and at times difficult, the sense of collegiality and respect in our multi - ethnic group was exceptional; something I've not experienced before or since. At times we struggled with difficult decisions, we argued, we disagreed, we laughed and we developed a deep respect for one another. The media criticism – to which we could not respond – served only to bring us closer together.

At our farewell I made these comments:

One of my favourite memories will be of our small lunch room with 6 or 8 people crowded in there with laughter, serious discussions, of Charles Paris slurping his noodles, Edith telling some great jokes, - there was more staff development going on there than in any session parachuted in from the east. We learned from each other, we argued, we challenged each other, we were enriched and it was fun. For that I thank you.

In our 1994 Christmas letter I wrote:
The dinner for those of us leaving the IRB was a time to say farewell not only to each other but also to mark the end of an era of hard work with a disparate yet cohesive, disciplined and conscientious group of truly remarkable colleagues. The wealth of experience, the

valued friendships, the recollection of struggles, and gifts of a pen and a New Jerusalem Bible will be cherished for years.

The New Jerusalem Bible had notes on inside the covers from colleagues:

I'm sure that you have noticed that the "imprimatur" for this Bible was given by Cardinal Basil Hume, a Cardinal of the Holy Roman Catholic Church… your ancestors should be turning over in their graves! (Charles Paris)

It is with some regret that I find myself writing in your Bible which I hope you will cherish as a symbol of the very high regard with which you are held; not only by myself but everyone who has had the distinct pleasure of working with you. Therein lies my regret because I am somewhat fearful that I may not experience such a privilege again…. (Lynda May Angus)

BC Ministry for Children & Families

At 57 years of age and with a mortgage, I needed a job. With my years of social work experience I assumed I'd have no difficulty finding work. Not so. Interviews were rare and after three months of searching I was offered a social work position by the BC Ministry for Children & Families. I started after Christmas in 1994; and after a few months in Chilliwack – an hour and 15 minute drive – I was transferred to Abbotsford and then in June 1995 to Surrey where I worked in the Whalley-Bridgeview area. Child welfare work in Surrey was different than in rural Manitoba. The increased use of drugs, poverty, addictions, loneliness, and isolation of some families presented lots stress and challenges for clients with few coping skills. For the last few years I assessed people wanting to become foster parents. In my last year I worked half time, job sharing with another social worker until I retired in January 2002.

Furball Alert

June, a social worker recently was at the home of one of her client families. This family had the cat's litter box just inside the door and one often stepped onto cat litter and/or feces on entering.

Invited to sit at the kitchen table she noticed one cat comfortably settled on the coffee table, the other, equally at ease, on the kitchen table. Shortly the kitchen table cat began retching and the father yelled "furballs, furballs" with the same words being echoed by mother. While announcing this to each other and to June, the cat proceeded to vomit on table and then moved aside to do whatever cats do after a furball attack.

Obviously experienced furballers, these folks knew exactly what to do. Dad got some paper towels wiped up the mess, and then in a casual manner held the towel close to his face, examined it and announced, "Yep, furballs." The discussion of family dynamics continued.
The cat slept.

Retirement

I worked at Vancouver City hall in the records department for a few months on an "as needed" basis. I was appointed to the provincial Employment and Assistance Appeal Panel (EAAT) in fall 2002 and worked for them periodically, hearing appeals of people unhappy with decisions regarding their income assistance. In fall 2007 I was appointed to the Property Assessment Review Panel (PARP), hearing cases of homeowners unsatisfied with the assessment of their property values. This work is all done in February and March each year. For a few years I did some foster home investigations for the Ministry for Children and Families on a contract basis.

Our volunteer involvement included about 8 years of Thursday nights at the Mission to Seafarers at Robert's Bank, working on the Board of the BC Mennonite Historical Society, the Board of the Canadian Mennonite Publishing Service and regular church committee involvement. Tena drove cancer patients for treatments and later worked in the

BC Cancer Society office in Tsawwassen. We delivered meals for Meals On Wheels in Ladner and I was on the MOW Board. I wrote articles for various publications: *Canadian Mennonite, Mennonite Mirror,* BC Mennonite Historical Society Newsletter and *Rhubarb.* I was a member of MCC BC's domestic violence advisory committee. I did a series of weekly sessions with recovering addicts at a treatment home in Burnaby.

From September to December 2002 Tena and I worked for Ten Thousand Villages in Petticodiac, New Bruinswick. This involved preparing crafts and artisan goods for sale, loading them onto a truck and each weekend heading out to a different community to hold a sale. In 2008 I began volunteering at the Ladner community police office.

Chapter 10. Writings, etc.

"One trouble about language is that people sometimes believe what you say, and you were only trying it out." William Stafford

Christmas letters

December 1991
Our year included Easter at Canon Beach, Oregon and a week in Ontario in May with Wendy & Kevin, another week in Manitoba with Andy & Kathy as well as Tena's mother.... In August Andy & Kathy moved to Brandon where Andy is attending university. In September Bev left for London, studying International Relations at the London School of Economics. In early October Tena had her left footed bunion removed....

December 2001
On February 28 the hanging lights started swinging at the Vancouver airport lounge as we experienced an earthquake while waiting to board our plane to Hanoi for a few weeks in Asia. Jake and Louise Buhler, international aid workers in Thailand and Vietnam, were gracious hosts and keen Scrabble competitors.

December 1993
For the first time since 1984 our family was together for Christmas '92.... Andy & Kathy will have Christmas in Brandon where Andy is at university and Kathy is a gambling addictions counselor. Wendy & Kevin will be in Toronto where Wendy continues at Ciba Vision and Kevin in sales. Bev will be coming home from

Ottawa where she does research for the Canadian Centre for Global Security.

December 1999
Clouds. We have a lot of them on southern BC…. We saw a few clouds and a lot of sun as we visited friends in the California - Arizona sun belt last March. Tena saw some British clouds when she spent a few weeks in London helping Bev move. We've had some beautiful cloudless days at family picnics when we've thrown lawn bowling balls. Henry has a bit more time to contemplate the clouds now that he's working half time.

January 2003
Our Christmas letter did not get written in the Advent season as has been our custom … there didn't seem to be time in our busy fall. In early September we left for Canada's east coast with stops in (to name a few) Vantage, Portage la Prairie, Carman, Mississauga, Lancaster and Plum Island before arriving in, New Brunswick. We were with Mennonite Central Committee's Ten Thousand Villages, based in Petiticodiac, N.B. until mid December.

December 2004
It was a trombone… creatively played by John Warkentin Jr. that helped celebrate my sister Hilda's and husband John Warkentin's fiftieth wedding anniversary. Numerous family members and friends joined in the celebration at Aldergrove's Bethel Mennonite Church, the same church where they were married. It was a valuable time of celebration, reminiscing and reunion with family and friends.

… we gathered at the Thresherman's Museum near Morden for a reunion of Tena's mother's family (the Friesens) in September; another meeting of friends and relatives from long ago. It was also the hottest day of the year in Manitoba, a day which concluded with a typical prairie evening thunderstorm. A friend in Manitoba we hadn't seen for a few years commented that I didn't look any worse than I used to, then quickly added that I didn't look any better either.

December 2005

Memories, celebrations and sadness describe the past year. In July we attended the 50th wedding celebrations of John & Anne Neufeld in Winnipeg. It was the first time since our parents moved from Manitoba to BC in the mid 1940's that we four siblings were all in Manitoba together. In spring we celebrated a significant birthday of Tena's by taking a cruise through the Panama Canal and back to Vancouver.

The celebrations were marred by the memories of the death due to cancer of Hilda's husband, John Warkentin. Last summer we celebrated John & Hilda's 50th wedding anniversary, now John is gone from among us. We commented to a friend that we're attending an increasing number of funerals and golden wedding anniversaries. He said that as long as we still knew the difference we were okay.

We were back in Winnipeg in fall for a conference recognizing the 25the anniversary of Canadian churches sponsoring South East Asian "boat people." This brought back memories of 20 years ago when we left our home and jobs in Manitoba for Thailand and work in a refugee camp, resulting in changes in our life which we could not have imagined.

December 2007

Christmas came early this year; Wendy was here from Toronto in November while Kevin stayed home to look after their business. Bev lives in Vancouver. Andrew and Susan are planning to be in Hawaii over Christmas. So, on a Monday night in November, we dined on turkey with all the trimmings, dessert and - to remind us of the gifts we used to get from Grandpa Suderman - chocolate turtles. No other gifts though, and that was fine. We don't need more stuff; people served by MCC and MEDA will benefit from our Christmas resources.

Christmas 2008

Change has come to Wendy & Kevin with a move from Mississauga to Antigonish, Nova Scotia. Wendy is now the Manager of Procurement Services at St. Francis Xavier University. Kevin continues with his home-based business (Morse Industrial) from their new home, much closer to his family home. Beverly is a Research Grants Facilitator at Simon Fraser University atop a mountain. Andrew and Susan manage to keep busy: Susan with Novartis, and Andrew as Director of Communications at the United Food and Commercial Workers Union in Vancouver, UFCW 1518. Tena and I? Well, if life has four seasons - the last being a season of rest - then maybe we're not old after all.

Sermons

We were often in churches that had no pastor and were led by lay (I hate that term) members. Despite little formal theology training - one course in church history at UBC - over the years requests or need resulted in me being asked to preach. Some sermon excerpts follows.

Frustrations with the Church
March 15, 1970, Westview Mennonite Brethren Church, Portage la Prairie, Manitoba. Subsequently printed in *The Canadian Mennonite.*

... *The first frustration is the church's reluctance and apparent inability to change. As an established institution… in society the church resists change… tradition and bureaucracy… prohibit innovation, ingenuity, originality and perhaps even the working of the Spirit. We insist that Christianity gives us freedom but we are not free enough to examine our traditions and practices with result that these become ends in themselves.*

A second frustration concerns the church's preoccupation with "spiritual matters" at the expense of concern for the total man. Church people conveniently compartmentalize their life into "spiritual" and "secular." This dichotomy implies that if the "spiritual life" is in order, nothing else matters. This philosophy results in churches devoting… efforts to getting people "converted" and conversion becomes and end in itself; and we have people committed to Christ but not to Christianity.

A third frustration is the "role playing" of church people. ... When Christians try to be nice people instead of real people they make the church repulsive and nauseating.

The church need to challenge me to re-examine my values, my ethics, my materialism, my whole way of life. I would like to see the church renewed so that it can finally break barriers between clergy and laity, between believers and doubters, between ethnic and social groups.

Love keeps no score of wrongs
December 26, 1971, Westview Mennonite Brethren Church, Portage la Prairie, Manitoba.

Love keeps no score of wrongs; the phrase keeps coming back to haunt me .... How do most of us react to disagreement, conflict, and problems in our marriages and families? Everything goes quite well for a while... then all of a sudden there's a blow- up between parent and child, between two children, or between husband and wife.

When this happens at our house I find myself getting angry at one of the kids and saying... "why do you always do that." The minute I say 'why do you always' I've admitted that I've been keeping score. Usually when there's a blow – up between husband and wife both are busily pulling out their scorecards listing the wrongs of the other party. Yet love keeps no score of wrongs.

Inaugural service, Portage Mennonite Church (October 16, 1977)
Why are we here? A number of responses readily emerge.
We are here because we share a common base in our faith in Jesus Christ.
We are here because we are friends and we care about each other.
We are here because we want to grow as Christians.

We are here because we want to provide our children with an opportunity to study, question, and to examine the call to follow Jesus as Lord.

We are here because we want to proclaim the triumphs of the Lord, in our lives and in the world.

We are here because we are prepared to take some risks in our faith, to work hard, and to claim His promise that He will bless us, whatever form that blessing may take.

We are here because we want to study, to pray, to be servants to each other, to grow in quality of life and to grow in numbers and to invite others to join us in our pilgrimage.

We are here because we want to make disciples of ourselves and of others

We are here because we are seekers, we have not arrived, not one of us.

We are here because we are free; we want to live life in the fullness, richness and joy that he has promised.

The opportunity for us is to live as building blocks, to give ourselves to God and to each other, to do God's will,
to be faithful, to serve,
to remain, or if necessary, to become humble,
to learn and to grow,
to be a community of the faithful,
to acknowledge Jesus as Lord,
and to have fun.

So, on this Sunday morning we stand together before God, acknowledging the smallness of our faith, concerned about the small number of people here, well aware that hard work lies ahead of us, afraid of failure and uneasy about success, confessing our sins, being forgiven and forgiving each other, wanting to be building blocks but being afraid to trust the builder, and finally, acknowledging that we are called to be faithful – to God and to each other – no more.

The Leap of Faith
November 20, 1977. Portage Mennonite Church.

A few months ago a few of us attended the Moscow circus in Winnipeg. The trapeze artist has to take some risks, his hands might slip, the timing might be a bit off, the rope might break, and down he would go. He has to trust that the other trapeze artist is swinging at the right time, ready to catch him. ... when we are standing on our secure platform a bar is swung out toward us, and this bar is always a threat. We are reluctant to leave our secure platform, our secure base. The bar is a challenge, an opportunity.

What are our securities? What are the things we are reluctant to leave, that we cling to? What is the one thing in your life that you do not want to do without? That is likely our security.

We are, all up on our platform of faith waiting for the bar to be swung to us we have to grab it and swing with it then let go of it and go flying through the air... but what if we fail?

That is the fear that keeps us from greatness – the fear of falling. When we risk... we are often going to be in a situation that is way over our heads, we will be out of our depth, we will need more power than we have. Growth involves risking, it comes as a result of the many minor and major decisions we make....

Maybe what Jesus is getting at is that faith and hard work go hand in hand; our responsibility is to do our duty, to be faithful – we are only servants – we don't nee dot expect any acclaim from the master, we have only done our duty.

Portage Mennonite Church
March 19, 1978.
In this world there are three scarce resources for which everyone is competing:
power, wealth and status. Jesus never sought the three resources for which people all over the world compete; he never sought power, wealth. The three temptations of Jesus were really temptations of power.

He came to serve others.

If you want to be the greatest, you must be the servant of all.

If you want to be first, you must be last.

When you are invited to a wedding, sit at the lowest place, not the highest.

Do not think of yourself more highly than you ought.

He came as a king, yet he came to serve.

Portage Mennonite Church.
June 18, 1978

One of the things we have to ask ourselves, is what is it about us as a group that makes our church life attractive to others? What is it about us that makes people want to come here? Or what is it that makes them want to stay away? And I have to ask myself what is it about me that makes people want to come – or stay away?

... The sense of belonging, the growth of a new community, an atmosphere of caring, does not just happen. It occurs when people have time for each other, when we stop talking (as I will very soon) and start listening to one another. What strategies do we need to develop within this group to ensure that sense of community and caring occurs? How free are we to ask each other for help?

Portage Mennonite Church.
September 3, 1978.

We have often distorted the meaning of the gospel by suggesting that the main reason for becoming a Christian is to get a ticket for a place in heaven. But God does not speak first about rewards but about responsibilities. We are not saved for a blissful future but for a difficult present.

... a Harvard psychologist studied the lives of 73 people who had been converted. Only one of the 73 showed any change in behaviour 37 had changed their speech forms, using the words "Lord Jesus Christ" and similar phrases in their speech, but their behaviour did not change. The remaining converts changed neither their behaviour patterns or their speech.

... we tend to keep the terms of discipleship hidden until a decision is made for Jesus. Our Lord never did this – the message He preached included the cross as well as the crown... he told his listeners to count the cost.

Power
December 31, 1978. Portage Mennonite Church
We sometimes tell our kids to "grow up" ... Jesus tells us to become like little children – he calls us to babyhood. Citizens of the kingdom will be like children. He calls us to flatten out the hierarchies and organization charts and forget them and ignore them as children do. The disciple relates to people as a child, and to a child the prime Minister and the milkman are equals.

There is no misunderstanding in what Jesus says – he flips the usual definition of greatness around completely. The pagans lord it over their subjects. Not so among you, says Jesus... in his kingdom greatness is measured by one's willingness to serve.

Jesus is not a king who barks orders to his generals, threatens his subjects, or uses brute force. He had no key spot in religious, economic or political structures of his day. Instead of pointing to the military or the king as examples of power, he points to the child.

So today let's take a second look at Tara and Krista and Julie as examples of the ideal kingdom citizens.

Forgiveness
January 6, 1980 Portage Mennonite Church
Several weeks ago I was in Brandon where I arranged to have lunch with Bruce Fraser, a good friend and former boss. In the course of our discussion Bruce asked me, quite out of the blue, if I had forgiven him yet. I was surprised since I didn't think I had anything to forgive; I was not aware of any reason why Bruce should ask for my forgiveness. He identified the

issue, we discussed it, and I assured him that I had not felt he committed any offence toward me. Bruce does not consider himself a Christian, yet here he was, asking me for forgiveness.

The church is to be a group in which the members communicate God's forgiveness to one another. Sometimes we play games when confronted with forgiveness.

Game #1. Sure I'll forgive, but first I'll teach him a thing or two. The intention here is to postpone forgiveness, to put some conditions on our forgiveness. "Teaching him a lesson" is not forgiveness, it's either a demand for justice or a groping for revenge. Forgiveness is a gift. A free gift of love.

Game #2. I'll forgive but only when he's made it right. I'll forgive when he's proved that he's really sorry. …if we use this approach we can avoid forgiving the other, we can feel superior and correct and criticize the other…. Jesus gave us the formula, 7 times in one day, or 70 x 7, take your pick.

Game #3. Yes I'll forgive and we'll pretend it never happened. This game allows us to avoid facing the real hurt and tension between you and the other. It lets you deny the anger….

Forgiveness is a gift we can give others, it is the act of love that will more than any other indicate our acceptance of the other, just as Christ accepted us.

If we don't forgive, there is no forgiveness for us, forgiveness from God does not come on any other terms.

Portage Mennonite Church January 6, 1980.
At our house, about a week ago, there was a discussion about my subject for this morning. Tena asked if I was going to give my annual sermon on the church; apparently (according to her) I've done this regularly in early January. Before I could respond to her suggestion, Bev commented that likely I would talk about the church, or to use her words, "you'll preach this

great sermon on the church and nothing will happen anyway." Some of you may want to talk to Bev about that later.

…Bev's comment confirms something people have said for along time – most sermons are really quite ineffective and don't result in any change. Maybe the problem is with the medium, with preaching or sermonizing.

Where have all the prophets gone?
January 26, 1992. Point Grey Inter Mennonite
I've been attending church for about 50 years now…. In all that time I don't remember any church having a prophet, or if they had a prophet they certainly did not call him a prophet.

Where are the prophets? Are they hiding in seminaries afraid to emerge lest the congregation run them out of town? I've asked a few pastors and where we can find prophets today and they become serenely defensive, saying that of course the pastors are the prophetic voice of the churches….

Bert was telling me the other day that the average life span of a pastor in a Baptist conference is two years. If pastors are prophets…then Baptists are not very tolerant of prophets, and I expect Mennonites are not far behind.

I attended part of the last MCC meeting where we have not only a resolutions committee but also a parliamentarian… is there a prophet somewhere in the midst of that?

… When the New Testament describes the gifts in the church, prophets are mentioned right up there with pastors and teachers…. Paul visits Philip the evangelist who had four daughters with the gift of prophecy. (Acts 21) Paul says it is prophecy that builds up the Christian community. Where are the prophets today? (Maybe churches are non-prophet organizations.)

The clergymen and theologians of our day? The deacons? The TV evangelists? The artists, poets and writers? Being an artist makes you an artist, not necessarily a prophet… being a pastor makes you a pastor, not necessarily a prophet.

So let me make a modest proposal, with apologies to Jonathon Swift: I would like to see the following advertisement in a church newspaper:

Opportunity.
Our congregation has an opening for a mature person of either sex and of any age for the position of congregational prophet….

You will interpret events of the times. You will speak to discrepancies between what you see in individual congregational life and what scripture teaches. You will have a deep love for your people. Your work will be lonely at times. Church boards, committees and pastors will be of little help to you since they are busy and preoccupied with their jobs, they may well see you as a threat.

You will have the ability to live above the need for praise; you will not fear criticism. You can anticipate being denounced, shunned, and supported from unexpected sources. Your work will be characterized by your humility and deep compassion for your people.

Training.
Formal theological training is not a requirement for this position, but is not necessarily a deterrent to suitability for the work. A sound knowledge and understanding of Scripture is essential. You will want to spend regular time in prayer and meditation; alone and with others.

Tenure
This is an indefinite term position. The successful candidate will be confirmed in one of two ways: by a consensus of the ladies group of this church, or by a similar group from a neighboring congregation affirming your call. You can be dismissed by the consensus of the ladies group after a review of your

work or upon the recommendation of a similar group from a neighbouring church.

Reporting.
At least four times a year you will report to the congregation ... you will communicate creatively and from the strength of your convictions. You will be expected to proclaim what is wrong with society and with this congregation. You will be an inspired and creative teacher. You will be granted time at any church function if you request it. You may speak to individuals or small groups; you may appear at any events and places including the workplaces and leisure activities of members.

Warning.
Since terrible acts have been committed through misguided zeal, you will be required to submit to a critique of your work at least every two years, or whenever the ladies group of the church requests a critique.

Salary.
None. Indebtedness to the congregation or anyone in it is likely to impede your ability to carry out your work. It is an advantage if you are not possessed of independent wealth or the pursuit thereof.

Applications including examples of your prophetic work may be submitted to the ladies group coordinator of this congregation.

And may God bless you.

Why are Non - Christians nicer than Christians?
13 March 1994, Point Grey Inter-Mennonite

...These examples indicate that sometimes the behaviour of Christians is noticeably worse than that of many non-Christians. Maybe we Christians aren't so different after all. We may have been seduced by society and have succumbed to the values of the world so that we are no longer distinguishable ....

C. S. Lewis address this dilemma on a personal level… if conversion to Christianity makes no difference in a person's outward actions, then we must suspect the conversion…. Jesus said by their fruits you shall know them. When Christians behave badly we make Christianity unbelievable….

… perhaps I need to re-examine my basic assumption. I assumed that Christians should be nicer than non-Christians. I may have done an injustice to non-Christians, to people of other faiths, and to God. My assumption limits God to working through Christians… I have no business putting limits on what God can do and through whom he can work… we should not be surprised when people of other faiths or of no particular faith are nicer people than Christians.

Jesus was rather blunt in the Sermon on the Mount, he talks about God's love for all humanity and God sending the rain on the just and unjust. THERE MUST BE NO LIMIT ON YOUR GOODNESS, AS YOU HEAVENLY FATHER'S GOODNESS KNOWS NO BOUNDS.

There's the measuring stick… is there a limit to our goodness? So when non- Christian colleagues show compassion and goodness that seems limitless, I need to give thanks for their compassion, to acknowledge that the spirit of God has touched them, and to review the bounds of my own goodness.

Parable of the Talents.
4 June 1994. PGIMF retreat.
The common interpretation of this parable is that God has given each of us abilities and talents…. We will be held accountable for how we use our resources. God will reward us for expanding them and using them to the fullest. In similar fashion, those who sit on their resources will be punished.

So what's the point of the talent story? … Go trade with this money till I return. But Jesus did not give his disciples money to trade with…. Jesus is saying to his disciples, I have given you my ideas and teachings about the kingdom, go trade with these ideas, get into business with those ideas. I've given you my teachings about anger, about how to treat your enemies, about speaking the truth, about not making a show of religion with pious talk ... about how to pray, about forgiveness, about possessions. ... Get to work with these ideas ... and when I return I'll want to know what you did with my teachings.

A man was going on a journey. He called his servants and to some he gave teachings on forgiveness, compassion and helping the poor. To others he gave the understanding of theological truths and the ability to teach .... To others he gave teachings on sharing and ... living simply. Some people took these concepts ... and ignored them.

Grant us the courage to get into business with these ideas.

Costly decisions and new growth.
4 June 1994. PGIMF
The interpretation usually given to the directive to take up our cross is that the cross is some suffering, inconvenience or tragedy foisted on us; an illness, a difficult teen, on obnoxious colleague, a disaster.... I don't think the cross is a hardship that we are forced into. The cross was not something forced on Jesus; he willingly went that way...

The cross was a difficult and costly venture. The cross is not an accident or tragedy that God send sour way; the cross is a deliberate choice.... The cross is a decision that costs us something.

A Kingdom of Priests. 1Peter 2: 1 – 10.
17 January 1999, PGIMF.
This calling to a new nationhood, to a royal priesthood, takes precedence over all other calls.... As disciples we come together as a holy nation to create a new community; a community with its own set of values – values often deviate from those of the dominant society. As... we come together

our structures and our agendas will appear upside down in contrast to other organizations.

Evangelical Christians are often criticized because of their weak doctrine of the church where the emphasis is much more on the conversion of individuals to personal faith in Christ with little attention paid to participation in the church....

The early Anabaptists had it right when they viewed the church as one priestly nation in which there could be no spiritual distinctions between members and clergy – each member assumes responsibility for the work of the Lord in the church and in the world.... In the kingdom we work together, not as lone rangers....

I said earlier that I had met royalty on two occasions – I need to correct that statement – I encounter royalty when I come here on Sunday mornings... whenever I meet other followers of Jesus, because we are a royal priesthood, a kingdom of priests, a chosen people....

Prayer
22 August 1999, PGIMF
There is another problem I have with prayer. Scripture tells us that God knows what we need before we ask. If God knows what we need, then why pray? Surely we are not required to tell God what we think we need. God knows it better than we ever will. God does not need our prayers, but God wants us to pray. So the purpose of prayer is obviously not to tell God what we need. Yet we are to come to God with all our needs. We need our prayers to God.

Maybe, just maybe, one of the purposes of coming to God with our needs is to examine them and to clarify the difference between our needs and our wants....
In C. S. Lewis's Letter to Malcolm he says: I have heard a man offer prayer for a sick person which really amounted to a diagnosis followed by advice to how God should teat the patient.... We are always completely known to God....

Unaffected Joy (Communion)
10 October 1999, PGIMF.
The early church did not eat together because somebody thought it would be a good symbol, a nice sign of being together. They ate together because they were together – whenever you are together with people you often eat together. A family eats together; a group of people on the job eat together. When you enjoy your guests you eat together. The reality of community is not symbolized, or dramatized, it is simply lived out ... it is celebrated.

We could spend a lot of time talking about the meaning of the bread and the wine ... but we should simply acknowledge that this is one way of saying Christ is truly among us ... but how this works is a mystery.... As C.S. Lewis wisely said, "The command, after all was to take and eat, not take and understand."

A Community of the Spirit. (Pentecost)
17June 2001, PGIMF.
What happened at Pentecost was the creation of a new covenant community. In contrast to individualism ... Pentecost marks the formation of a new community.... To be saved meant to participate in this new social reality, created by the spirit of Christ.

Jesus, Pharisees and Rules.
17 August 2003 PGIMF
My image of Pharisees is seldom, if ever, positive. I see them as legalistic, rule- bound, prideful about their piety, hypocritical, self-righteous. (And of course I'm not at all like that.) My negative characterization of Pharisees distorts my view Judaism and the beginnings of Christianity. The problem Jesus had with the Pharisees was not one of belief, but of practice.

The religious leaders of Jesus day were doing their best to retain the true faith. The Pharisees were serious about their faith, they tried t follow the rules and they had lots of them. They were not rigid and unfeeling legalists.…

Many of us… would have joined the Pharisees. The ides of translating our faith into daily practice would have excited us. They were part of a renewal movement; they were the evangelicals of the day. They meditated on the word. They established rules for following the religious teachings… they had strong traditional family values. Maybe we need to listen to the message of the gospels as if we were Pharisees, for we are the ones who have created institutions and program sot express our faith.

Eugene Peterson notes that when people get their hands on religion one of the first things they do is use it as an for instrument for controlling others… the church's history of manipulating and controlling others is long and tedious.

Jesus approach is far more costly than rulebook ethics. According to Jesus you don't always have to keep the rules – he certainly didn't.

Ascension Day.
23 May 2004.
I remember one Ascension Day traveling with a colleague to Rosthern Junior College. When we were finished our business and were leaving the students were heading for the chapel. My colleague asked why Mennonites were going to church on a Thursday morning. I said it was Ascension Day. She became quite upset… as a devout Catholic she had forgotten about Ascension Day and had not gone to morning mass. During the day she commented on this omission several times, we talked about why Mennonites celebrated Ascension Day. … when she dropped me off at home she asked to use our phone and called various Catholic churches until she found one that had an evening mass which she could attend.

Rules; Love goes Ungiven.
31 July 2005

Each of us has our own history with church rules…. Like the Pharisees we often want clear answers, we want to be certain about what is right and what is wrong.

We want rules to make things clear. So we have people searching the Bible to see if they should watch TV, buy an SUV, marry someone, attend Bible school, join the army…. This kind of searching the Bible scares me… I worry because some people claim to understand the Bible so well – for these folks the rules are clear and laid out in Scripture. The Bible is not a rulebook; it speaks to a lot of issues, but not in a rulebook sort of way.

Many of us, had we lived in Jesus day, would have admired, followed and joined the Pharisees. …There's a lot of haggling over stuff that doesn't matter as much as we think, while love goes ungiven.

That last line – we haggle over rules while love goes ungiven – is a powerful indictment of the rule makers. We haggle over little stuff while love goes ungiven.

Love is the identity marker of Christians…. Everyone who loves is a child of God and loves God.

Jesus in the Temple
31 December 2006 PGIMF

What puzzles me is how did Jesus learn enough about the Jewish faith to engage in dialogue with the teachers in the temple. Samuel was taken to the temple at an early age and grew up there…. We don't know where Jesus got his religious knowledge – was he taught at home?

This makes me wonder about religious training of children and Sunday School… and how much Jesus might have benefited from it. Yet SS was not created till the 1780's in England. It was started to provide reading and writing skills to children who worked as chimney sweeps. The Bible was the textbook.

Since SS didn't start till the 1700's, how did Christianity survive without it? How was faith transmitted?

Today we have youth ministers and even children's ministers; we have camps for children, child evangelism, children's clubs, vacation Bible school and SS.

Are these children's programs our way of admitting that we lack the ability to communicate our faith to adults? Recently I read about a 2003 Southern Baptist study that found that 88% of children from evangelical homes in the US leave church around the time they leave high school... many of these young adults never return to church.

Belonging, Behaving and Believing.
29 April 2007. Edited version printed in *Canadian Mennonite*, 27 April 2009.
At a recent dinner discussion Tena and I had with Mark Davison, an Anglican priest, Mark said there are three components to the Christian faith: believing, behaving and belonging.

He went on to say we usually arrange them in the wrong order – we want people to believe in Jesus, then to behave in a Christ-like way, then to join the church and belong.

Believe, behave and belong. That's a formula for selling heavenly life insurance.

When we ask people to first believe we're asking for an intellectual assent to some propositions, to some words.

Jesus tells the religious leaders "set my words aside just look at what I've done, if you're going to kill me, for which of my miracles are you going to kill me?

When Jesus called his disciples, he never gave them a test or examination about their beliefs, about their theology, about their faith. He didn't ask them if they believed the 10 commandments ad Mosaic law. He simply said, "Follow me."

Hang out with me for a while,
Join up with me.
Watch what I do.

I wonder what a church growth strategy would look like if we said to people, come hang out with us for a while, see what we're about. Or we could even take a more dangerous route and say, like Jesus did, look at my life, at the things I've done and then decide about the Christian life. If my deeds are my credentials, that gets quite personal, it's scary.

Jesus told people to believe in him; "repent and believe the good news," and "whoever believes shall not perish but have ever lasting life."

The context of these statements is important. The difficulty for Jews of Jesus day was profound. They were under Roman military occupation hoping for a messiah to deliver them. Jesus comes along and announces he's the one. But he isn't worried about the Romans. It's no big deal if a soldier wants you to carry his pack for a mile – you carry it for two. If your enemy is hungry, feed him. Repay evil with good.

This is not the kind of Messiah they expected or wanted. They wanted a military leader to drive the Roman out. For Jews of his day to believe in Jesus as the Messiah required a radical shift that was beyond their comprehension. It required a total re-thinking of everything they believed. That's what Jesus called for when he asked people to repent and believe in him. Change your behaviour totally. Re-jig your thinking because you have it all wrong.

That's what conversion in Jesus day required. But conversion doesn't require that from us today. And Alan Kreider in his 2000 book, *The Change of Conversion and the Origin of Christendom*, notes that the church of the first few centuries made a huge issue of behaviour before getting to the belonging and behaving parts.

But conversion doesn't require that of us today. We don't ask people to reject their fundamental thinking and behaviour. Instead we say, "Believe this and you're saved." That's the **heavenly insurance** formula. But Jesus didn't give them a simple formula. He said if you want follow me, start over.

Our preoccupation with correct belief is excessive… we have creeds, statements of faith, and covenants, all designed to keep us on the straight and narrow. If we all just believe the same thing… everything will be fine.

When potential pastors are being interviewed, they are asked such questions as:
Do you believe the Bible?
Is it inerrant?
Do you believe in the Trinity?
Do you believe in a literal hell…?
Do you believe women in ministry is biblical?

But rather than focusing on the candidate's theology, the person's behaviour should come under scrutiny. Your deeds are your credentials, so tell us what you've done. Candidates should be asked what they've done to alleviate suffering in the world….

On another occasion, James and John wanted to call down fire from heaven on the Samaritans and Jesus said no. Just because people believe differently than you – that's no reason to condemn them. That's not how to treat people with whom you disagree.

Jesus said of the Pharisees: they have all the right doctrine and they believe all the right stuff, but where is it going to get them? The important thing is to live like Christ not to believe in a prescribed creed or statements of faith.

Love is more important than doctrine. The purpose of Christianity is not to discuss the details of theology, but to minister to human misery.

Yet if I insist on a "belong, behave, believe" order, I am simply replacing one formula with another. Maybe what is important is that all three happen, and continue to happen....

Hang out with us for a while, see what we're about, get to know us, see what we do. That was the way of one who said, "*My deeds are my credentials.*"

An Uninvited Guest.
17 June 2007. PGIMF
How do you deal with uninvited guests who interrupt your well-planned and orderly proceedings?

A number of years ago Eugene Peterson said that the word "evangelism" is pejorative, it has too many negative connotations in our world and we need a new term to replace it. He suggested we replace "evangelism" with the word hospitality. Now that's a revolutionary concept. Hospitality might capture more fully what Jesus meant. The question might not be how evangelistic are you, but how hospitable are you?

Move off the Page.
21 October 2007
I was taught to believe in a literal, every word inspired view of Scripture. The thinking goes something like this: since Scripture is inspired by God it is inerrant; and because Scripture is inspired and inerrant, it alone has final authority. Since God is perfect and he inspired Scripture the text must also be perfect. People with this view think of the Bible as if God faxed it to the writers.

Before the modern period, Jews, Christians and Muslims all relished highly allegorical interpretations of Scripture. The word of God was infinite and could not be tied down to a single interpretation.

The preoccupation with literal truth is a product of the scientific revolution, when reason became important and mythology was no longer regarded as a valid path to knowledge.

In our day there is a tendency to read scriptures for accurate information – part of our scientific orientation – so that the Bible becomes a holy encyclopedia in which the faithful look up facts about God... we are now reading the scriptures instead of listening to them....

We need to develop a way of reading where we assume that not all texts carry the same weight but they add to the richness of the whole.

Jesus did something remarkable which eventually got him killed: he rewrote scripture. To move from an eye for an eye law to loving your enemies is a remarkable rewriting.

... Anabaptists emphasized the role of the Holy Spirit in interpreting scripture, not a wooden interpretation of the words....

Faith equals Obedience: functional atheists.
1 June 2008, PGIMF.
The Old Testament simply talks about obedience, not faith. The OT hardly mentions the word faith. I checked a concordance and the word "faith" appears about 4 times in the entire OT.

This puzzled me so I emailed some friends and asked if by emphasizing faith we have it backwards; are we merely selling heavenly life insurance? To my surprise they all said yes, we've got it backwards and we're selling heavenly life insurance. Rebecca says we separate what we believe from what we do with the result that many western Christians are functional atheists....

Jesus says there's a basic question we need to ask anyone who claims to speak for God.... We need to ask how is your faith evident in your life? What kind of results – fruits – do you see?

In the sermon on the Mount Jesus says whoever hears these words **and puts them into practice** and teaches these commands will be called great in the kingdom of heaven.

Show me your Glory.
8 February 2009, PGIMF.
The concept of glory is prominent in Scripture. C S. Lewis warns that we not get too preoccupied with the potential of glory of the hereafter, of heaven. He says we need to look at the glory of God in our neighbour. This is where the weight - or burden – of glory comes in.

Desmond Tutu told a black servant lady during S. Africa's apartheid days that if anyone asked her who she was, she should say: I am God's partner, God's representative because I am created in the image of God. Tutu says each of us is a God carrier and we need to hold each other in awe and reverence... seek the glory of God in each person you encounter.

Some years ago the late missionary Jake Loewen, speaking in this church... said the closest we'll ever get to God is the person sitting right beside you. That was a startling thought... maybe he meant that we need to see each other as God sees us: we need to see the divine light – the spark of the divine – the glory shining through each other.

Job
8 August 2010
How do we respond to people in distress? How do we reconcile the presence of illness, tragedy and evil with a loving God? When there's an accident, an unexpected death, a marriage breakdown, we often hear comments like "they were such nice people, such great neighbours" – implying, like Job's friends, that bad things should not happen to nice people. But

they do. When tragedy strikes someone will give us all the stock answers, like Job's friends.

Eugene Peterson says that when bad things happen, religious friends, like Job's friends, can be the worst. They're often fixers. They're so convinced they know the truth. They're so confident they can fix you up, if only you'll listen. Job's friends were not able to fix him.

Our friend Alice was dying of cancer and a clergyman – a fixer told her she needed more faith and she would be healed. A saintly person, she asked: How do I get more faith?

General Articles

Child Abuse – some Cultural and Religious Observations.
February 1984. (Excerpts from a speech to an interagency group, Winkler, Manitoba.)

What we have in the Mennonite communities in southern Manitoba is a religious and cultural group that has, over many years, developed patterns of family life. They (Mennonites) are a cultural group that has an alleged high view of family life, a group that values children and frowns on marital separation, divorce and family breakups.

While these observations may be accurate for the group as a whole, there are notable exceptions. Those of who work as social control agents… are expected to pick up on the casualties of our society… to fix them and to send them back as normal, healthy productive individuals.

In working with the failures of the Mennonite families and community we see that there are some distortions that Mennonites as a group hold related to the values of Christianity, family life… and people helping each other.

It is important to look art some of the religious beliefs and teachings of Mennonites since religion.. can be used for good purposes or for horrendous purposes.

When we deal with child abuse and incest we are dealing with an anomaly; that is, something that doesn't fit the customary order of things. Child abuse is still the exception, not the rule, and that is important to keep in mind. When confronted with deviance societies face three options: a) the behaviour can be ignored, b) the behaviour can be condemned, or c) the behaviour can be deliberately confronted and seen in a new way.... To a large degree the problems of abuse and incest have been left to the social control agents to cope with – the social workers, police, mental health professionals, teachers and clergymen.

What we find is that many abusing families use religious based sanctions or rationalizations for their behaviour. The father or mother... beating their children say they are only doing what is biblically correct; "If I don't beat my children they'll go to hell." ...He is establishing himself as the head of the house and master of his property and – wives and children are part of that property.

This behaviour is allegedly sanctioned by the church... what the churches seem to be saying is that it is better for the mother and children to stay home and be abused rather than for them to leave their husband. In one family the mother said she didn't think the abuse was harmful because her daughter had not yet become pregnant... the teenage daughter who had been sexually abused by the father is accused of breaking up the family and sending dad to jail. She is victimized repeatedly.

So what we have is a closed family system, a system in which great efforts are made to hide the abuse, to keep it within the family.... the first step that needs to be taken is to allow and encourage the law to take its course. We are faced with a situation where a law has been broken, a crime has been committed; police investigations need to be completed and the course of criminal justice followed.

The victim of abuse needs to realize she was indeed the victim – of incompetent and inept parenting and of a poor family relationship. She must hear this not only from her counselor… but from her own parents who have to acknowledge responsibility for their behaviour.

… we have a history in southern Manitoba of professionals and agencies hiding clients on each other. Where agencies are protecting abusive families, where agencies are refusing to deal with the abuse ands neglect that they know exists… this gets expressed in a very professional way, "I think I can help this family in a nice way," or "I don't think in this case it'll be necessary to go to the police." When this happens… we have become part of the problem and it is time to step back and take another look.

I have suggested three things, firstly we find out what function the incest serves within the family, secondly… that we involve religious leaders and the churches in dealing with some of these problems. I know some of you are concerned about confidentiality… my experience is that confidentiality usually means that everyone in the community knows what's going on except the professionals. Thirdly, agencies represented here form a child abuse and neglect committee to begin working together in planning treatment strategies for these families.

One Lady's Childhood.
(A client wrote about of her difficult childhood, 1970)

I too was an unwanted unloved child because I was a mentally diseased child as long as I can remember. My parents were very strict people, very proud, never believed in a "mental or nervous" disease, they beat me because I couldn't control my fear, they laughed and jeered at it and made me mind my four younger brothers and sisters for 10 to 12 hours with strict instructions to look after them very carefully and the promise of a terrible licking

*if I had those shameful notions again that I was afraid – choking
up when tension built up – my terror suppressed.*

*I was hidden from company because they were so ashamed of me
and I overheard my parents telling each other that they didn't
know where they had sinned so much as to be punished by having
a child like me. They agreed to pray that I would die – hence my
fear doubled and redoubled for I had a terrible fear of death and
of God and of the terrible fires that all bad children will be thrown
in after death. I know what it means to soundly plea and beg for
a kind look from a mother I worshipped - how often I so deeply
yearned from my mother's work-worn hands. But I grew up – she
never kissed me, never hugged me once in all my childhood or
teenage years and she never stopped blaming me when I couldn't
keep my illness from her.*

Words from the Western Mountains.
In the early 1990's I wrote a series of articles for the
Mennonite Mirror.

The Wedding
Even though lateness is not uncommon at such events and
might even be considered fashionable, this wedding had a
leisurely delay about it. Some guests arrived after the service
began, bowing in prayer before taking their seats. Finally the
bride and groom were in their appointed places and the music
faded to signal the end of the preliminaries.

Hymns were sung, prayers seeking God's blessing were made,
and the young couple was reminded of their responsibility
to each other, their families, their faith, and society. Ideally,
they were told, they should seek to achieve ones in spirit and
in body. As weddings go, it was a colourful. impressive, and
beautiful ceremony.

Flavourful aromas son drifted into the sanctuary, confirm-
ing the destination of the ladies who left during the latter
part of the service. We were served an abundant meal;

the food was tasty and varied as one might expect at any Mennonite wedding.

The master of ceremonies introduced the head table, welcomed guests, singled out those who had come from afar, told a few jokes and did all the things required of him.

The high-pitched clinking of spoon on cup demanded a show of newly wed affection and all eyes turned to the couple. The mother of the bride was not amused and whispered something to her daughter. Words between bride and groom, then he leaned over, moved her veil gently and kissed her on the cheek. Video and flash cameras captured the moment; the crowd applauded in approval thirsting for a repeat performance.

The religious faith of the group was a major concern of the older people present. Many important traditions were being lost and the faith was being eroded. Young people were adopting the behaviour and dress style of Canadian society. Alcohol consumption, formerly forbidden, was now common at weddings; one glance at the amply stocked bar confirmed this.

The food was traditional, tasty, and reflected a well organized kitchen of which any congregation could be proud. We were told this crowd was conservative and there likely would be no dancing, but at other weddings where there were more youth, dancing was not uncommon.

The older people had concerns about their youth: they no longer came to worship regularly, they were caught up in the competitive world of education, careers, and business. Children were still being instructed in the faith, but as young adults they left the fold and there was hope that they might someday return. But many valued traditions were being lost.

Conservative dress was giving way to popular Canadian styles. For reasons of convenience and acceptance by the larger society, these changes were almost inevitable but unfortunate. The loss of the old ways was to be mourned, as was the loss of the mother tongue. While older people spoke with marked accents, the youth spoke only English. In one generation the language of the ancestors was being lost.

Regular worship was important, the elders said, to maintain connections to others, to the larger community. Failure to become part of the community of faith would lead to selfishness and individualism. People seemed too busy to take time to worship regularly. God was not given a rightful place in people's lives. It was sad, they said, and shoulders shrugged in impotent resignation.

It could have been any Mennonite wedding; but the saris, turbans, and curried foods reminded us that we were at a late 20th century West Coast Sikh wedding.

An Unlikely Prophet

It is doubtful that during his lifetime anyone considered Mr. Driediger a prophet. He seemed a serious man, at times almost morose. He possessed a wry sense of humour and a scowl; both were used almost interchangeably. He was not particularly active in the Mennonite church though he attended regularly; he would not have been described as religious. On occasion he walked out during a sermon. He spoke clearly and used fewer words than others to say the same thing. Some said he smoked.

It was a mid-1950's summer evening after a workday, in the bunkhouse, with a few cohorts and some teenagers, that he made what may have been his only prophetic utterance.

There was an intense discussion about the future of the German language in the church. The youths, impulsively wise and to the surprise of no one, advocated the immediate and total shift to English, for all the good youthful reasons.

The argument continued… a few adults ventured their thoughts. Mr. Driediger was quiet. He frowned, took a deep breath, and said in Low German: "If we lose the German language we lose much more than a language."

This brought challenges and demands for elaboration from the youths. Mr. Driediger said it again, word for word, with no explanation. There are obviously times when prophets do not defend or explain themselves; this was one of those sacred moments....

Were our prophet to look at the B. C. Mennonite churches today, the truth of his words would be confirmed: the German language is virtually extinct. And more than a language has been lost.

Words can readily be translated in to another language.... Our prophet's concern went beyond translation of words; he knew that the German language provided a protective barrier... that made it difficult for a variety of influences to affect the church. The German language insulated Mennonites from the theological extremes that periodically swept across North America....

The issue our prophet addressed was not the German/ English language... languages are but symbols to retain and convey concepts. Our prophet saw churches which could not make the language change and at the same time ensure that the essence of our forefathers understanding of Scripture was maintained....

He saw the dangers, he issued a warning, and he was, as is not uncommon with prophets, ignored.

Friendships are not Transferable

The previous year's vacation in B.C.'s coastal region was all that any family could hope for: warm days, mosquito-free cool nights, and spectacular mountain scenery.... A few inquiries brought Dad a job offer at a salary that was high by prairie standards… The rental truck was loaded, farewells were said and another family joined the flock of prairie refugees in B.C.

The initial enthusiasm of this adventure faded… more time spent in vehicles: for work shopping, church, medical needs, recreation or visiting friends. Mom had no friends to call or visit…. Isolation, loneliness, and feelings of rootlessness set in. There was little to connect them to their prairie past…. She longed for the open prairie, for space, for distance from people, for closeness to the right people….

The kids spent their first summer back in Manitoba. On their first day back in B. C. they confronted their parents with their blunt declaration…. We don't want to live here anymore. Months later mother would admit that she liked what the kids said, it rang true, but she had not dared say it.

Theirs is not an isolated story… even in B.C. man does not live by mild winters and beautiful scenery alone.

Appendix

Someone's sitting in the shade today because someone planted a tree a long time ago. (Warren Buffet)

Neufeld, a common Mennonite family name, appeared for the first time in the Danzig (Gdansk, Poland) Mennonite church records in 1694. The name originally referred to land reclaimed from the sea. The Neufeld name was common among the Mennonite congregations of Danzig, Prussia and Russia from where it spread to the United States, Canada and South America. It has a Flemish background. The *Universal Biography* lists two teachers of philosophy at Danzig: George H. Neufeld (d. 1673) and Konrad N. Neufeld (d. 1656), both sons of George N. Neufeld.

The Mennonites
Originally called Anabaptists or "rebaptizers" because of their belief in adult rather than child baptisms, they originated in Switzerland in 1925, maintaining that Luther, Zwingli and other reformers had not gone far enough in distancing themselves from the Roman Catholicism. The Anabaptists broke from Zwingli's church and are sometimes described as neither Protestant nor Catholic.

The first adult baptism took place in Zurich, Switzerland, in January 1525. Political authorities declared the movement illegal, but the rebaptizers flourished, practicing their faith in secret. In a few years, there were groups of baptizers throughout Europe.

What made the Anabaptists a distinctive reform movement was their interpretation of common Christian teachings. They emphasized the importance of following the teachings of Jesus, especially the Sermon on the Mount, the importance of the church and a life of discipleship. Menno Simons, a former Catholic priest became the leader of the Dutch Anabaptists and it's his name that identifies his followers – Mennonites.

Due to persecution many Mennonites moved to the Vistula Delta along the Baltic Sea and the Danzig area (now Poland) in the 1530's. Here they became highly literate and educated; they became known for their hard work, farm productivity and reclaiming swamps for farmland. This was the beginning of many years of searching for a haven, a place where they could follow their faith and raise their families in peace.

In the mid 1700's growing military preparations in Europe and a shortage of land coincided with an invitation from Catherine II inviting German and other European settlers to occupy lands seized from the Turks in Southern Russia. The Mennonite migration to Russia in 1780's despite initial difficulties, resulted in Mennonite flourishing there for over a century. Most farms were 176 acre plots, some became wealthy estate owners, owning an average of 238 acres. The colonies were largely self-governing.

The Molotschna colony, founded in 1803 where my parents resided had 1,200 families in 58 villages by 1835. In 1918 there were still 75,000 Mennonites living in Ukraine. It was a well-developed socio-economic group with a mutual aid program, homes for the aged, hospitals, orphanages, mental hospitals, a special school for deaf-mutes, a girls school, and a business school. By 1914 there were 400 elementary schools, 13 high schools, two teacher's colleges, four trade schools and a Bible school. (C.J. Dyck. p.138) The Mennonites established what became known as the "Mennonite commonwealth" of Russia. It was a prosperous and successful place.

With the shortage of farmland in Russia, the 1870's saw the first wave of Mennonites coming to Canada and USA from Ukraine. An exodus occurred in the early 1920's; prompted by the 1917 Bolshevik revolution and loss of freedoms. Changing Canadian economic conditions resulted in political opposition to more immigrants; by 1928 only 511 Mennonites were admitted to Canada. By 1929 there were 10,000 Mennonites in Moscow seeking to leave, but Canada said no to more immigrants.

The German government granted temporary admission to a 5,700 refugees in 1929, including the extended Neufeld clan. Despite the obstacles to emigration to Canada 1,123 of this group were allowed to come to Canada, including Herman and Sara Neufeld, and their young daughter Hilda. Most of the others found their way to Brazil and so we have numerous relatives in Curitba, Brazil.

My Father: Herman Wilhelm Neufeld
(31May1893 – 11February1982)

Herman was born in the Mennonite village of Ohrloff, in the Molotschna area of Ukraine. His parents were Wilhelm Herman Neufeld (1860 - 1938) and Katherina Warkentin (1864 - 1911). Life in Ohrloff was comfortable; there was a secondary school, an orderly village government, church, youth activities, farm work, choirs to join and vacations in Crimea.

Herman completed high school in Ohrloff and worked on the farm that had been in the family for generations. Herman's mother died in 1910 and his father married a widow, Margaret Epp, on 1 March 1914. Mrs. Epp brought two children into the marriage: Martin Epp, who died in 1916 and Margaret Epp, who later married Mr. Jacob Rogalsky in Brazil. The Rogalsky's moved to Virgil, Ontario and in the early 1980's to Surrey, B.C. to live with their son John Rogalsky. Herman's father died in Brazil in about 1946.

Herman Neufeld was baptized in the Lichtenau Mennonite church in Ohrloff in spring 1914. That November he was conscripted by the "White" as opposed to the "Red" army and served with the Red Cross; the alternative to military service. He was sent to the Caucasus region as part of the 127th division and in early 1915 his unit was sent to Batum in the Russian province of Georgia; later they were deployed to Turkey on the eastern Black Sea.

In late 1916, while still with the Red Cross, Herman contracted typhus and was hospitalized for six weeks. Around the same time he contracted "Kopfrose" a shingle–like condition affecting the nerves in the forehead accompanied by strong headaches and a rash on the scalp that led to permanent loss of hair – the reason Herman was bald. He got permission to go home for four weeks, a ten-day trip one way.

In discussing his WWI service, Herman pointed out that he was eligible for Canadian veteran's benefits due to being part of the allied "White" Russian effort. Dad never applied for these benefits since he believed it was wrong, as a Christian pacifist, to benefit financially from war. Some of his colleagues from WWI applied for and received Canadian veteran's benefits. (Herman's account of his military service appears below.)

My Mother: Sarah Bartel (21 December 1899 - 12 September 1972)

Sara was born to Johan Heinrich Bartel (from Gnadenfeld) and Sarah Friesen Bartel on Rosenhof- Brodsky estate at Taurida, 50km from Melitopel, Ukraine. Taurida included the Crimean peninsula and the mainland between the lower Dnieper River and the Black Sea and the Sea of Azov. Sara was the middle child of three; her older brother Hans (John) died as a young lad of diptheria. Her younger sister Anna Bartel (d. 18 May, 1972) worked as a nurse and married Dr. Alexander Sartschenko. (sp??) The Sartschenko family immigrated to Pennsylvania in the post WWII era. They have three children: Nina Sartschenko, Frieda (and Nial) Crawford and Rudy (and Lucy) Schenk.

Sara's family was wealthy, her father was an estate owner, and the children were home-schooled by a tutor. Sara's father died in October 1918 at the age of 44. After several years Sara's mother married Isaak Enns from Steinfeld. About five years after Isaak Enns's death Sara's mother married Cornelius Janzen and they moved to his home in the village of Ohrloff where Sara attended the local girls school. Mom witnessed the shooting of her stepfather, Cornelius Janzen by the Makhnov bandits in 1918.

Herman and Sara met when Sara's family moved to Ohrloff in 1917. They were engaged on 8 August 1920. Engagement at the time was a formal event, a celebration was held at the bride's parental home with a clergyman delivering a brief sermon. Herman and Sara were married on 25 April 1921 in Ohrloff. Herman and Sara lived with his parents; an experience Mom didn't talk about much but it must have been difficult since she commented that it was not a good idea for newly-weds to live with their parents.

Sara was quite sickly and frequently visited the doctor. In 1925 Herman and Sara both had malaria and were quite ill. On 19 April 1927 their first child, Willi, was born. It was a difficult birth and Sara told Herman they should thank God for him – Dad said that was the first time he had prayed aloud.

The post revolution Bolshevik era was difficult, characterized by lawlessness and chaos. In this power vacuum armed gangs stole, raped, and pillaged at will. I recall mother describing how one band arrived at her parental home, demanding a certain amount of grain. They swept the granaries to try to meet the demands, but were unable to provide enough grain. As a consequence Sara's step-father, Cornelius Janzen was shot in front of his family in 1918. Earlier Sara's stepbrother had also been murdered.

Herman described how 20 men from Ohrloff took up arms to protect their village, providing night patrol and shooting at approaching bandits; they had weapons instruction from a German officer. Dad said and they had a prayer service before chasing the bandits; shot at them but Dad does not know if any were hit, neither did he say that he was part of the armed militia; I suspect he was.

As the Stalinist regime increased in power there were more arrests, disappearances and deportations to Siberia. Herman and other extended family members were warned that they were to be arrested next. On 7 November 1929 they left in a matter of hours via train from Lichtenau for Moscow and then traveled to Germany on the last train of immigrants allowed out of Russia in that era. This journey has been documented in the film "And When They Shall Ask." Sara's mother remained in Ukraine along with Sara's sister Anna.

From the extended Neufeld family in the German refugee camp, only two families were allowed into Canada: Herman, Sara with infant daughter Hilda, as well as the Enns family: Herman's sister Katherina (Tina) and her husband Aron Enns. The Enns's settled in the Steinbach area.

The other three extended families in the refugee camp included Herman's father and stepmother, Herman's brother Heinrich Neufeld and family and Herman's sister Maria and her husband Rev. David Koop and family. These relatives were rejected by Canadian medical authorities on grounds of an eye condition; trachoma. Herman vigorously denied this, claiming the Canadian doctors were tired and didn't want to process any more immigrants. These families immigrated to Brazil and eventually settled in Curitiba where they developed a flourishing dairy and milk processing industry. Rev. David Koop was the Bishop of the Mennonite church in Curitiba; I recall him visiting us in Aldergrove in 1949 in connection with the Mennonite World Conference and again in 1961.

Herman, Sarah and daughter Hilda (b. 21 June 1929) - their son Willi died in the Hammerstein refugee camp in Germany - boarded the Cunard liner *Auriana* in Hamburg, Germany on 4 April 1930. Herman was 37, Sarah 30 and Hilda 10 months old. They traveled via Southhampton, England, and were billeted in England for a few weeks due to health problems of some passengers. The *Auriana* carried 500 passengers on this voyage and arrived at Halifax's Pier 21 on April 13, 1930. It marked their arrival in a new and unknown place.

Mom's Story

(by Sara Bartel Neufeld, written 4 May 1969, translated from German)

My parents were Johan and Sara Bartel (nee Friesen) I was born in the year 1899 at Brodsky (Brotsky) where we had a home tutor. My brother Hans (John) was the oldest, he and I had one year of schooling from this teacher. Then my parents moved to Tiegerweide where we attended the village school. My brother Hans died of diptheria so only my sister Anna and I were left.

In October 1908 my father died at age 44. After several years my mother married Isaak Enns from Steinfeld. After his death mother remained single for about five years then she married a man from Ohrloff. That's where I lived in my teenage years, they were good years.

My (step) father, Corneilius Janzen had 10 children; Mary and Elizabeth and I were of similar ages and Mary was the oldest. In 1918 I attended catechism classes and was baptized that year on confession of my faith By Bishop J. Wiens, who later lived at Herschel, Saskatchewan, Canada. Bishop Wiens had also been my teacher in the village school.

Here my dear husband and I learned to know and love each other. On 8 August 1920 we had our engagement celebration, Rev. Ediger, a teacher at the local high school had the sermon. These were unsettled times and at the end of August my Herman had to leave our village. Despite this separation we were reunited and on 25 April 1921 we were married. We were married in the Ohrloff church by Bishop J. Wiens; my (step) sister Elizabeth Janzen married Peter Toews the same day, it was a double wedding. The wedding sermon text was Luke 10/39.

The times were serious and unstable. In our first year there was food shortage where we barely had enough to eat and sometimes we couldn't satisfy our appetites. We lived with my parent's-in-law, Wilhelm Neufelds. I was sickly and often had to see the doctor. In Ohrloff I had appendix surgery.

In 1925 we both had a serious case of malaria fever. Later my mother-in-law also got this fever. Our Lord wanted us to yield to him completely.

In 1927 on April 19 our first child was born, our son Willi. It was a very difficult birth but our God was gracious and helped. God be praised. On 21 June 1929 our daughter Hilda was born.

In 1929 on 7 November we left Ohrloff and the Molotschna region. The Makhnov bandits were active in our area and shot many people in our villages including (step) father Cornelius Janzen who was hit by a deadly bullet. Earlier stepbrother Kornelius Janzen was also murdered.

My mother and stepfather Aron Dyck from Wernersdorf (he was mother's fourth husband) stayed behind. They were not allowed to stay in their home. Mother died in 1931, on June 20. My sister Anna cared for her till she died. Mother died with a strong faith and we want to live so that we'll see each other in heaven.

We got to Moscow and from there to Germany. When we arrived in Germany both children, Willie and Hilda, from all the exertions of the journey were very sick. Willi had pneumonia; he had a relapse and his heart wasn't strong enough. The Lord took the lamb to heaven. He died on 2 February 1930 and was buried on 6 February in Hammerstein, Germany. The sermon was by brother-in-law David Koop (later from Brazil) his text was Psalm 16:6. Hilda had an inflammation in her throat but regained her health, thanks to God.

In April 1930 we arrived in Canada. 1931, on 26 April our daughter Margaret was born in Steinbach Manitoba. Son

Hans (John) on 12 November 1933 in Winnipeg at Concordia hospital, son Heinrich (Henry) on 26 January 1937 also at Concordia hospital.

Here in Canada we moved a lot, first in Manitoba then in 1945 we came to BC, living first in Sardis, then in March 1946 we moved here to Aldergrove where we still live, first on a strawberry farm, then on 1 August 1959 we moved into our new home, near the church (24752 56th Avenue) Where we failed, may God in his grace forgive us. On 25 April we had our 48th wedding anniversary and we are deeply grateful that we are healthy even though we have some maladies related to aging. Herman had a slight heart attack in January, but thanks to God he's better now. I've had 5 operations, often serious nosebleeds, but my Saviour always helped me. God be praised.

Late January 1970. Now we're almost a month into the new year. On 21 December I had my 70th birthday. We're healthy, thanks be to God. God has been gracious; we want to trust him for the future.

A Short Story of My Life by Herman W. Neufeld, 1893 – 1982 (written in German about 1975, translated by Peter Bartel)

I was born on May 31st, 1893. My parents were Wilhelm Herman Neufeld and Katharina, nee Warkentin. I attended elementary school in Ohrloff, Molotschna, where my parents operated my grandparents farm. I attended High School for 3 years. My mother died in March 1910. I helped my father in the farm work.

On March 1st, 1914, my father married the widow Margaretha Epp, who had 2 children: Mrs. J. (Jake) Rogalsky and Martin, who died in 1916. Around Easter of 1914 I started to attend baptism preparation and was baptized on the confession of my faith on Pentecost by Elder B. Epp.

In August 1914 war with Germany started. It was November when I was called to enlist. There were 50 of us who were sent to the Caucasus area and we became part of the Red Cross service in Tiflis. I became part of the 3rd division and was sent to the Batum *area after New Years of 1915. We experienced many things and God was gracious to protect us during this time. I became the assistant to a chauffeur and had to open and close the doors of the cars, crank the engine, for the elite who used our services.*

In May we were sent to the Turkish town of Trapezunt near the Black Sea. 1916 at Christmas I contracted typhus and Kopfrose (shingles) and was in the hospital for 6 weeks. By God's grace I regained my health again. Many thanks to the head nurse, Lady Siegel from Riga. Her husband was the commander of the 127th division. I was allowed to go home on furlough and it took 10 days to get home. I stayed there for 4 weeks. In Oct. of 1917, I was given another furlough and never returned to the front. We were in the middle of a revolution and everything was falling apart.

I got to know my future wife as a young girl. We were engaged on August the 8th, 1920 and the wedding was on April the 25th, 1921. Because of the difficult times, we seldom had enough to eat – many days not even a whole piece of bread.

On the 7th of November 1929 we left our home with our 2 children (Willi and Hilda). We left everything behind and were glad that, with the help of God, we arrived in Germany on the 7th of December of that year. On Feb. 2, our Willi died and we buried him in Hammerstein on the 6th. Our brother-in-law (Rev David Koop) led the funeral service.

On April 1st, we left Hamburg and arrived in Winnipeg, Canada on the 14th of April. We moved a lot in Manitoba. In '42 we moved from Headingly to Springstein where people showered us with love and acceptance. We joined this congregation and were richly blessed.

In 1945 we moved to BC, and arrived in Chilliwack on Jan. 5th. In 1946 we moved to Aldergrove where we bought 10 acres of bush, cleared it and planted strawberries. The Lord blessed our work and we were able to grow spiritually, as well. We joined the church there. I have often been unfaithful to my Lord but he always led me back. To him belongs all the honor and glory.

50th Anniversary: Memories from our Marriage

(written by Herman W. Neufeld in 1972)

We would like to remember today, how wonderful God has been to us and praise Him because it has all been pure grace that we can celebrate this event today. On Aug. the 8th, 1920 at our engagement, high school teacher, Sam Ediger was the speaker. It was the time of the revolution, where the Red and White armies were in full battle.

At the end of August of 1920, I was drafted into the White army. When the White army began to withdraw from our area, 6 of us decided to defect and walk away while on duty as night watchmen. We walked 20 miles to reach home and arrived safely because we had changed clothes to look like wagon drivers. We were stopped by the Red army officials but were allowed to go on. We arrived home in the middle of the night. The house was full of Red soldiers because the White army had been driven out of the region right down to the Black Sea. Only a few thousand of them escaped by boat out of the Crimean Peninsula.

We were not mistreated because this part of the army was a regular division, not like a band of renegades, who arrived later and caused so much havoc. Our father was allowed to keep one of 8 horses, because it was lame. He also kept 2 of his 10 cows. In 1921, a little more order was established and so we decided to get married on April 25th. Elder Jacob Wiens officiated in the church at Ohrloff. The meal was a simple "Faspa" and there were no presents, because everything had been stolen. There was nothing to buy in the stores anyway and no money. The devaluation of the currency was rampant.

One evening in Nov of 1921, I was arrested with 4 others. We were transported to Halbstadt under heavy guard and placed into the cellar in the house of G. Harder, a minister. A room that was 20 by 30 feet had to hold more than 60 men. The night before that 5 men were shot, who were all known to us. Phil. Cornies, the vice president of the Verband (association) was arrested with me. (The reason for my arrest: I was accused of shooting a man in a Russian village about 40 miles away – it was not true.)

The first night I was called up 5 times to be interviewed. Only a beast can be so horrible as they were. A revolver was stuck into my mouth with the threat that I would be shot like a dog if I did not confess. When I arrived back in the basement, they were having a prayer meeting led by Phil. Cornies. There were Russians, Bulgarians, Catholics and Lutherans and we all prayed to the ONE God and he helped us through this. After many days, we were loaded onto wagons that were guarded on each side by a rider and 2 soldiers for each 4 prisoners. We drove through the night and arrived in Waldheim as the sun rose. We were again put into a basement.

My dear wife visited me daily in Halbstadt and a few times we were allowed to talk under supervision. Now we were about 40 miles from home. Next morning we were called, one by one, and told that we could go home. We did not wait a minute, and my friend Jash Doerksen and I set out right away. We had to look after our own food – they didn't feed anyone.

At Landskrone we had lunch at the John Thiessens, Jash Doerksen's parents' brother-in-law. Soon we were on our way again because it was far and dangerous. At Fuerstenwerder, our relatives: Abr. Tiessens, Doerksens' sister and her husband and my dear wife met us. We started out immediately and got as far as Tiegerweide. At uncle and aunt P. Heidebrechts we fed the horses and ate and arrived in Ohrloff after dark.

The next day my brother Heinrich came and said that I had to disappear. There was an opportunity to go with relatives to visit my aunt Susanna Neufeld, my mother's sister. They had been driven from their estate and were living in the village of Alexanderfeld, about 65 miles south of us. I arrived just in time. The men had been arrested the day before but I could stay because I was from a different village. I was allowed to bring them food every day. After three weeks there I received word that I would be able to come home and I didn't waste any time and came home safely.

But how did things look there? My father had been arrested in the meantime and all the grain had been taken. I was not arrested. Jash Doerksen had left for the Charkowsche area. We had no grain for flour but we had good feed for the cows that gave plenty of milk.

In January of 1922 it was bad – little food and the currency was devaluing daily. A pound of butter cost 1.5 million ruble. The money was worthless. For example: Dad had a 10 h.p. motor for the threshing machine which he sold for 35 million ruble and I received 3 million to take it to the city. It took me 3 days for the round trip of 40 miles. We had agreed that I should try to buy grain for the money, if possible. I was able to buy 7 bushels of oats and 15 lbs. Sunflower oil. The oats were milled at the windmill and that was the flour for our bread. We seldom had enough to be full. It was rationed so it would last. Our heavenly father provided. We received a package from our father's sister in California, the David Klassens.

The first Fordson tractors arrived, and because I had been a chauffeur from 1915-18, I was given a job with the co-operative. We received a few clothes, some rice, sugar and cocoa as our wages. We also received our daily meals from the villages in which we were working. The harvest was average and we were required to hand in a portion of our harvest. We were able to keep enough to see us through. The Red government became more stable and we were able to work. The land was divided into 16 hectare (32 acres) parcels per family. Father and we had 32 hectares, 4 horses and 4 milk cows. In 1925, five of us, including brother-in-law David Koop and his father, bought a new Fordson for 1800 ruble. I went by train to Alexandrowsk to pick it up and from then on we started to do custom plowing.

We also bought a large threshing machine with which I did custom work for 8 weeks. As wages we received a tenth of the harvested grain. This carried on till 1928, when the village was organized into a commune in which all families were to work together under the supervision of an overseer. Late in 1928, I was still able to sell the tractor.

Starting in 1929, everything was communal. We did not like that. We saw that the whole change was difficult and took much time. They were experimenting. Soon we heard that in one village, some had sold all their stuff and traveled to Moscow to apply for a passport and a visa. After the harvest in 1929, we also started to plan a similar move.

Those who had larger properties (estates) were moved off so that the officials could move in. Across the road from us were Johann Wiebes, whose children (son-in-law) and family were put out of their place. He was veterinarian. We became acquainted with him, and one night he came to the window, woke us and said that I should wake my brother Henry right away and tell him to disappear immediately.

My brother hiked through the forest to P. Nickels in Tiege. The next day I went there and brought him some things and 200 rubles. The Nickels took him to the station the next day and he went to Moscow. It was the end of October. I went to town and sold 2 cows and 2 horses. We sold the furniture secretly. We dared not sell the house.

On Nov 7th the villagers had a meeting. My cousin Heinz Warkentin and I also went. Our veterinary neighbour was there and he came over to us and asked whether we had some tobacco. We said Yes. He said he would give us cigarettes for some of our tobacco, this seemed strange. He handed us a tin. When we opened it we found a note with the words "Get away, now." When the meeting started we both left and returned home and he got his wagon ready.

We quickly packed a few things, dressed our two children (Willi and Hilda) and drove to Lichtenau, 4 miles away, where my mother's sister, Maria lived. She died in Brazil in 1971. She was single. I had arranged with my father that we would leave for the station at Prischib early on the 4th day. This was a trip of 25 miles and brought us to the direct rail line to Moscow. I had about 700 rubles. I went to Muensterberg and said goodbye to aunt Suzanna, where I had been in hiding (in Alexanderfeld).

I had hired the shepherd of Lichtenau to drive us to the station and we left on the appointed day. Aunt Maria came with us. We left at 4 a.m. and arrived at the station at daybreak. We unloaded and put Sarah and the family into the waiting room. As it got lighter, I saw a wagon coming from the direction we had just travelled. I recognized our horses and now it meant that we had to act. Four men sat in the baggage room, talking to each other. I went and asked which of them was the boss. I asked the one who identified himself, how much it would cost to ship the baggage which we had to Moscow. They looked at each other and the boss said: "25 rubles." I paid him the money out of my wallet.

When I returned to the waiting room, it was full of people who were waiting for the train. Outside the familiar wagon was getting closer. I went back to these guys and asked whether they would get me the tickets, they said yes. I paid the 370 rubles and had my tickets within 15 minutes. When our wagon arrived they helped with the baggage. We were the first ones to get on the train when it arrived, but over half had to remain behind because there was little room. We were all able to get on.

After 2 days and nights of travel we arrived in Moscow – but now what? None of us had ever been in this city. My brother-in-law Aaron Enns and I went to find out what we could do. Suddenly we saw Peter Regier, from our village, who had been sent by my brother Henry to help us. He had rented a house, a distance of 40 miles away, and we had to go by train. We could not take our baggage with us on the train. We hired two wagons for 150 rubles and I drove with the our baggage, leaving at about 10:00 a.m; the others went by train.

We arrived in Kljasma station when it was getting dark. Where to now? Then I saw Henry Willms, from Tiege, greeted him and inquired about the whereabouts of (brother) Henry. He told me that his son had just come from there and that he would send someone along to show us the way. In an hour we found the place – God led all the way again. The drivers fed the animals and then returned. When we had settled in we wanted to rest.

At 12 midnight someone is at the door. When we opened, there were 4 policemen. We had to show our papers and they looked into every room, where the family was sleeping on the floor because there were no beds. They left and did not bother us again. The next day we had to register at the police station and entered into a register. Brother-in-law Aaron Enns drove the 6 miles by train to the police. The other men went into the forest to gather some wood. When A. Enns returned, all had been registered except myself. I had 24 hrs. to do that.

The next day I took the first train to Pushkin? and got into line. There were 20 ahead of me. When it was my turn, I gave them my book and papers. They looked at them, said NO and gave everything back to me. I had no chance to talk to them. I got into line again and started to pray. When it was my turn again, I handed in my book and papers and did not know what else to do. He wanted to return the papers again. It came to me to say that my name was in Ukrainian. He took the papers again and stamped them. (this means: My name was "Roman" in Ukrainian, in Russian it was "German"; it was the latter one I had entered in the book.) When I came home, there was much joy. The next night the police came again to check things out. In the 28 days that we were there, they came 21 times. One night they took a Peter Regier, 19 years old, and we never saw him again.

My brother Henry, who had been there for 3 weeks, was working secretly at setting up lists to use to apply for passports. Our only document was our wedding certificate from the year 1921 – and this was November 1929. Around the 20th of Nov. we heard that at two railway stations closer to Moscow, all were arrested at night, loaded into freight cars and driven away. Many young men were put into prison and horribly beaten.

On the 25th of November, the policeman came at breakfast time and told us that we could go and apply for our passports and emigrate. We did not believe them. The lists were in a house six houses away. Henry went there and found out that it was true that Germany had accepted us. We were allowed to apply for passports, which would cost us 50 rubles per family. The registration papers all needed to be handed in. Dad became ill. In a few days the first train left. Therefore, there was hope.

On the 5th of December we got on a train with all that we had. We traveled one and a half days to the border. On the way we had to hand over all our Russian money to the agents, who were also very interested in American Dollars. I had one, which I also handed over, so that we came over the border with no money at all.

In Estonia, the children received cocoa and white bread, which we had not eaten for a long time. When we crossed the border, the Russian agents got off the train and were replaced by Estonian ones. These were very nice and intelligent. Spontaneously, the group broke into the well-known song: "Now thank we all our God..."

From Riga, on the Baltic Sea, we traveled south in a German train. On the (German) border we all had to bathe and our clothes were disinfected. Naked we had to stand and wait. I held Willi on my arm and Mama had Hilda. Then we traveled on to Hammerstein.

After another clean-up we were put into barrack #3, (officer barracks). Our parents, Greta and Henry and D. Koops were put into a communal barrack. We were about 3000 persons. We were all given food and drink and warm blankets. The boss of the "Lager" (refugee camp) was a Major Fuchs. We were not allowed to leave this camp. I got work keeping the disinfection kettle going and for that we received double rations of bread and sugar.

Christmas was approaching. Everyone received something and the children were very happy about the toys and sweets they received. We had worship services. There were @ 5000 persons here, among them a few Lutherans and Catholics. The toilets had to be *cleaned and emptied every day. This was done by the men while the women helped in the kitchen. We received clothes. The New Year started with a worship service as well.*

Our Willie was not well. In the middle of Jan. 1930 we had to take him to the hospital in the camp. Many children died. Six men made the coffins. On the 2nd of Feb. we had to say goodbye to our Willie. It was difficult. The funeral was on the 6th of Feb. at which our uncle, David Koop, read Ps. 16:6 and 73:23-26. Willie was #121, and each grave is marked with a white cross with name and number on it. We have a picture.

In the middle of Feb. (1930) a Canadian Medical Commission came and sought smaller families. We were part of that group and made it. On March 1, we said farewell to our parents and family and were brought to Moelln, which was 50 km from Hamburg. We were put up in a school for officers. Our uncle Henry was not in Hammerstein, but in Breslau, near Berlin. In Moelln, our group had shrunk a lot and we were divided into smaller units for the trip. Food was also provided.

Since our Russian passports were for only 3 months, every family that was emigrating was photographed and received a new German passport. On May 30th we went to the wharf in Hamburg. Peter Klassen from Ontario was the Missions worker there and accompanied us onto a small ship. There were 130 of us. He came with us across the channel, up the Thames River as far as London.

At the station in London we transferred to double-decker buses with the driver on the left side, who brought us to another station where we boarded the train and in the morning we got to Southampton. After another thorough checkup, we were transferred to the Cunard ship "Aurania". I ate only one meal on that boat because I became seasick. In seven days we arrived in Halifax.

Arthur Unruh, from Winnipeg, came to greet us at the harbour. Before we transferred to the train, we had to sign a paper promising that we would not go to any of the cities in Canada but rather settle on a farm. Mama and Hilda did not miss a meal on the boat. In Winnipeg we were met by Rev. C.N. Hiebert who now lives in California. We arrived at the C.N. railway station on April 14, 1930.

From the station we traveled to Chortitz, near Steinbach, Manitoba. We went to the farm of Is. Baergs, arriving on the Thursday before Easter. They were just beginning seeding time. Now we, especially I, had to learn everything from scratch. All my life I had worked with horses, but these animals would not listen to me at all. But I did know how to clean the barn and milk cows.

Starting May 1, we took work with Abr. Wiens, about 2 miles from the Baergs. Mama had to milk mornings and evenings and then clean house, bake and cook for them the rest of the time. Mrs. Wiens was always working with her. This lasted till Oct. 1930 and we received $200.00. Work was not very hard but everything had to be learned anew. On Sundays we went along to the MB church for worship.

In the beginning of May, Aaron Enns's and children, our siblings, arrived in Steinbach. Our parents, Henry, aunt Mary and Dav. Koops stayed in Moelln. That same month, the Conservative Party came to power in Canada who closed the doors to further immigrants. That is why the rest of the family remained in Germany. There was no hope of coming to America.

RED CROSS SERVICE – WW I.
by Herman W. Neufeld, 1973. (translated from German by Peter Bartel.)

It is strange, that we, the first of 50 Mennonites in Tiflis (who had taken alternative service instead of joining the Russian Army) were celebrating Christmas in an army camp in 1914 (the name is unclear from fathers notes). Around the tree we sang songs, had a sermon from Corn. Wall. Our General and his wife had joined us.

Before New Year of 1915, five of us: Peter Goosen, Jacob Hildebrand, David Unruh, Wilhelm Cornies and I, were sent to the 3rd division of the Red Cross. Our whole division consisted of 250 men. Our commander was General Plemhamikow, and there were doctors, medical students, nurses, a tactical section with trucks and what else was necessary. Near Tiflis, I do not remember the exact location, we were organized into a unit and put into barracks.

At New Year we arrived in Batum, where we heard our first cannons. The front was only 12 (verst) miles from the city. For several days our unit was under the open sky. Then we had to move on along a solid cobblestone road along the Chorocha river, which flowed past Batum into the Black Sea. About 40 miles upstream we made camp. Because only 4 men were placed in each tent, a large tent city grew out of the ground. There was also a large tent for the sick, one for the drugstore, one for the officers and one for the commander. The tactical part for all the horses, wagons, and ambulances was a distance away.

W. Cornies and I were placed with the medical crew. We learned how to deal with the injured and bandage their wounds. The guards and the officers treated us very well. We did not have to participate in the military drills. When it was our turn to guard, we were sent to watch the horses that they did not run away and had enough feed. We did not have to carry guns. When our ruler, Alexej Nikolai arrived, we were sent to the kitchen to peel potatoes while the others had to line up for an inspection parade.

Walking uphill was always difficult because there were no roads, only paths. After a while we caught up with an artillery unit. The 3-inch cannons had been taken apart and loaded onto the saddles of 6 donkeys. We walked from 8 AM, had a break at noon and then continued. At dusk we nearly reached the ridge from where we heard the noise of several cannons. At this level we had about 4 feet of snow. Under a fir tree we shoveled all the snow away, to the bare earth with small shovels. There was no water. We looked for dry branches, made a fire and melted some of the snow in order to have something warm in our stomachs.

At dawn we were awakened because we had fallen asleep in a sitting position and the noise of the rifles was close enough. Our soldiers, who were Cossacks from the Kuban, had received orders to storm the enemy lines. Our night lodging was about 50 feet from the ridge. Around 9 the first casualties arrived. The doctor called me to help him bandage the wounds. The first one had his upper leg splintered by a bullet. The doctor showed me how I needed to hold the foot so he could, on command, pull the leg in order to put on a splint. We had no anesthetics. As I began to pull, the man started screaming, no roaring. For me, as a beginner, it was too much. Later, the doctor told me that I had caused him a lot of trouble. As I regained consciousness, I was lying on branches under a fir tree. That day we had 136 persons with wounds. When I had fully recovered, I noticed that my toes had frozen.

I was given 18 lightly hurt men that I had to look after while I accompanied them to the field hospital and handed them over to the staff there. We arrived when it was already dark and I was also given a bed in the hospital, my boots were cut open to release the pressure on my swollen feet. The mountain, on which we were stationed, was called the 15th border post from Batum.

Dr. Collman from Riga treated my feet. Since he had studied with Dr. Pinker, who was our doctor in the hospital in Ohrloff, I was given a lot of privileges and he kept me there for 3 weeks. He then arranged for me to be stationed in the office of the business part of our unit.

In August of 1915, our Red Cross division was given its first car chauffeured by Michailow? from Petersburg. He needed an assistant to crank the car and to clean it. I got to know him and asked him to take me as his helper. I offered him 100 rubel to teach me to become a driver. They did not want to let me go from my job in the office. Finally, I was allowed to go and for me it was the start of another life. I washed cars, polished all the chrome and was the official door opener and closer for the V.I.P.s, naturally I had to stand at attention with my hand on my visor.

We made frequent trips to Batum where we often waited till 2 A.M. till the officers returned. In those times, Michailow taught me all about how a motor works. He had excellent books on how to take care of and repair a car. In this way I was able to see more of the surrounding area and had a lot more freedom than in the tight quarters in the tent of the organization. After 3 months, Michailow allowed me to drive the car to the river for a wash. I first had to fetch the water in pails. Slowly I learned all about becoming a driver and whatever else I needed to know.

One night, on our way home, Michailow asked his boss for a holiday. No, he said curtly, there is no one who could drive the car. He pointed to me and said: Hermann can drive. So I was sent to Tiflis to do the drivers test and received the 2 category because I was not a specialist. When I came back, Michailow went on holidays and I never saw him again. Kudaew, who was from the Kuban, became my assistant. Early in April 1916 our army occupied Trapezond and the next day we moved into the central part of the city.

Six new ambulances arrived – called Jeffreys (?) Now we had a lot of driving to do for the officials, the doctors and the nurses. A large hospital was set up. Our 3rd division of the Red Cross unit was serving with the 127th infantry division but our section with the vehicles remained in town. We were 18 men and a cook. The ambulances had to get the wounded from the front. The head nurse of the unit, the wife of the commander of the 127th division, Mrs. Siegel, was strict and intelligent. I had to drive her a lot and got to know her.

In the fall of 1916 I asked to go on leave and it was arranged that I would go around Christmas time. It did not happen because I came down with typhus fever of the bowels. I can't remember anything of the first three weeks. When I was allowed to eat again, Mrs. Siegel often brought me some wine and other goodies late in the evening. After 6 weeks I had mostly recovered. One morning the doctor came and asked me whether I had headaches. No, I said. My head was red and I came down with (Kopfrose) shingles *which lengthened my stay for another 2 weeks. Finally, I was allowed to go home for my holidays in Jan. 1917.*

Wilh. Cornies also received leave. So we traveled as far as Batum on the boat. After 10 days of travel, on the train, we arrived at home. It was my first homecoming since Nov. 1914. The 4 weeks passed very quickly. Meanwhile, the Tsar had been deposed in Feb. (1917). Many things had changed while I was gone. I got a Fiat to drive. Often, we were stopped by the soldiers who commandeered us to drive them. Many officers and generals were released of their command but general Siegel stayed with his soldiers because they loved him and appreciated his wife as head nurse. I received letters from her from Riga in the spring of 1918. In Nov. 1917 I took another 4 week leave.

In the Rostov train station, where I had to change trains, someone stole one of my suitcases with all my best clothes. After a week at home, I heard that one could buy release papers from the army for 25 rubles in Berdjansk in the Borksky Natschralnic. I went there and returned 4 days later with my release papers and stayed at home. How many dangers one has been in – in all, God's protecting hands were with me.

Neufeld Immigration Interview, Pier 21, Halifax (April 1930)

Questions asked of Herman and Sara Neufeld by Canadian immigration in Halifax. (Source: National Archives of Canada, Microfilm: T-14825, Volume 7, page number 37.) Some spelling is phonetic.

Place of birth: *Orlow/Protzky/Orlow*: Herman/Sarah/Hilda

Country of Birth: *Russia*

Race or people: *German*

Ever refused entry to or deported from Canada? *No*

Do you intend to reside permanently in Canada? *Yes*

Can you read? *Yes/Yes/No*

What language? *German*

By whom was passage paid? *Menn. Aid Wpg.*

What trade or occupation did you follow in your own country? *Farming/Housewife/Child*

If destined to relative, friend or employer, state which and give name and full address.
Aunt: Margaret Fast, Port Rowan Ontario BB#3 (Sara's Aunt-in-law)

Give name, relationship and address of your nearest relative in the country from which you came. If a wife or children are to follow later to Canada, give names and ages?
Father-in law: Aron Dicek, (Dueck?) Wernersdorf, Russia. (Sara's father/Hilde's grandfather)

Have you or any of your family ever been:
Mentally defective? *No*
Physically defective? *No*
Tubercular? *No*

Passport – number and date of issue? *1799, Molln, 7-3-30*

Money in possession belonging to passenger? *None*

Traveling in land on? *CN*

Action taken and civil examiner? *Landed immigrant stamp.*

The End